Contents

Introduction to the book.   Page 4

Chapter 1:   Page 7
Understanding your feelings.
(Why do I feel so bad?)

Chapter 2:   Page 39
Doing things that make you feel better.
(I can't be bothered doing anything)

Chapter 3:   Page 81
Looking at things differently.
(Why does everything always go wrong?)

Chapter 4:   Page 111
Building inner confidence.
(I'm not good enough)

Chapter 5:   Page 141
How to fix almost everything
in 4 easy steps.

Chapter 6:   Page 169
The things you do that mess you up -
and how to stop doing them.

Chapter 7:   Page 195
Are you strong enough to keep
your temper?

Chapter 8:   Page 229
10 things you can do to feel happier
straight away.

Introduction

Welcome to Living Life to the Full.

I'm Professor Chris Williams, a medical doctor who works in mental health and well-being in Glasgow. I've been working for the last 20 years looking at ways of helping people improve their lives.

We can all sometimes feel down or fed up, stressed or worried, or that we aren't good enough. However, there are things you can do to make positive changes in each of these areas. It also involves rediscovering the things you already do that are good for you- and how to build these in your life.

I work using a talking treatment called cognitive behavioural therapy- or CBT. It is often offered to help people with low mood or stress. It can help prevent problems such as these developing in the first place. Because of this it is increasingly being offered as a way of helping people learn key skills that can give them a growing sense of control over how they feel and react. These are skills that can last a lifetime.

The course is a series of chapters and linked FREE ONLINE course modules that are often also taught in classroom settings by trainers working the health, social care or voluntary sector settings. The classes have been evaluated in research, which has shown that the course improves problems of low mood and anxiety.

I firmly believe that skills such as these can make a real difference to any of our lives. There are no quick fixes, and to really get good at using the skills will take practice, - but who doesn't need to learn how to be calmer, more confident and in control, happier and someone others turn to for answers?

Discover more at: www.llttf.com

Information for educators and practitioners: www.fiveareas.com

Course resources for young people:
www.WeEatElephants.com
(ages 5-12 years)

www.llttfyp.com
for young people aged 13-18.

If you need more help: Reach out and tell someone- a colleague, neighbour, doctor, or trusted family member or friend. Get the help you need. Don't suffer in silence.

As you read the book, you can print off any linked worksheets from www.llttf.com to allow you to practice the skills you are learning (free registration).
Look out for this BUTTON to highlight these free resources.

Introduction to Chapter 1

All of us from time to time feel happy - glad, even joyful. When we feel like this it's a great feeling isn't it?

But sometimes we feel bad. Down, low, sad, stressed, anxious, worried, panicky, angry or embarrassed.

Did you know we feel like we do for a reason? That's what this chapter is about. It provides you with the keys to understanding you and how you feel.

Have you ever had a bad cold? You notice the runny nose and sore throat, the itchy eyes and the aches, pains and coughs. How we feel in our bodies also affects how we feel emotionally, what we think, and how we react and relate to others. So, when we have that cold, we might feel emotionally numbed, and not able to enjoy things as before. It might feel harder to think things through, give a talk in class, or make important decisions. If we were feeling ill like that, we might find we choose to wear different clothes at home, or eat or drink different foods. We also might relate to others differently - making sure that our illness is clearly communicated to them.

This illustrates an important point. That how we feel is affected by our bodies, thoughts, and actions as well as what goes on around us.

This chapter will help you discover what makes you tick – and how you can gain a sense of control over how you feel and how you act. You can't change what you don't know- and by the end of this chapter you'll know a lot more about what makes you feel good – or bad.

Chapter 1

UNDERSTANDING YOUR FEELINGS

(Why do I feel so bad?)

SOMEONE CLOSE
IS REALLY ILL

Friends hate me GOT
DUMPED

Best
friend
ignored
me

LOST
my JOB

Being
ill

Failed
the
exam

ALL
ALONE

Got
kicked
off the
team

GOT
CRITICISED

GOT NO
MONEY

No-one to
talk to

Too much
to do

BEING
BULLIED

You feel bad because you're in a vicious cycle

The way you feel is affected by things that happen to you. Like the things on the opposite page. Those things are all outside of you. Sometimes, you can change what's happening outside, but often, you can't do much about them.

And when you allow them to affect your mood, the vicious cycle kicks in and you feel worse and worse and worse…

Vicious cycles spin by affecting five areas of your life.

Turn over to see how it works

Forgot my sister's birthday
SOMEONE CLOSE IS REALLY ILL
Friends hate me
GOT DUMPED
Lost my job
Best friend ignored me
ALTERED THINKING
Being ill
I'M USELESS
Failed the exam
ALL ALONE
Got kicked off the team
GOT NO MONEY
GOT CRITICISED
No-one to talk to
Too much to do
BEING BULLIED

First, an outside event affects you

When something happens, you naturally notice it and think about it. If you forget your sister's birthday, for example, you may think "I'm useless!". This is called **Altered Thinking.**

Altered thinking can set off a chain reaction inside you that affects the way you feel and what you do.

When your altered thinking is negative (like "I'm useless"), the vicious cycle is triggered and you can end up really down, not getting out of bed and even feeling ill.

Let's see the Vicious
Cycle in action

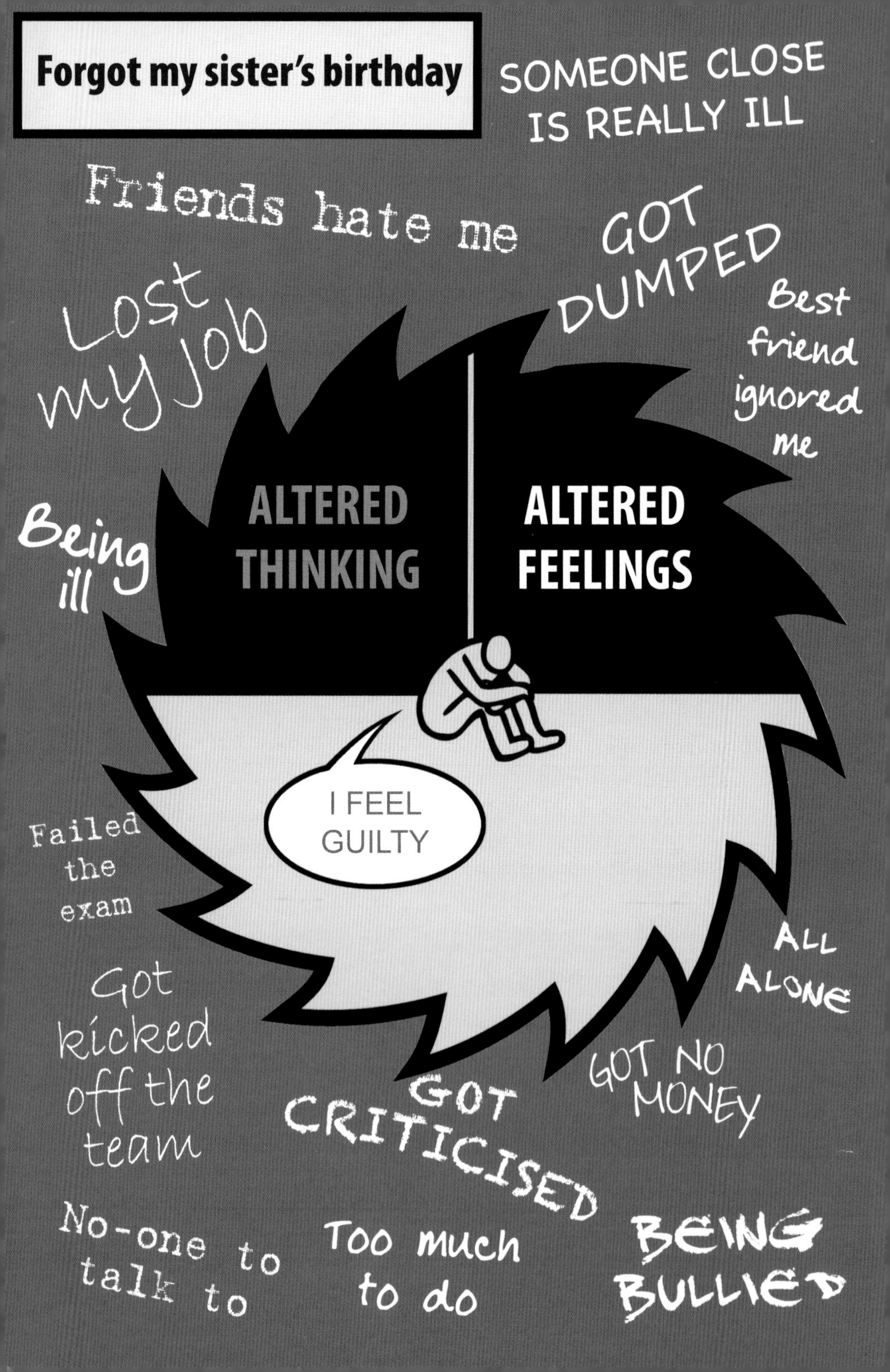

Altered thinking leads to altered feelings

If you think "I'm useless!" you're going to feel pretty low, sad or guilty.

Maybe you feel as if you've let her down, or you might feel guilty because you know you should have been more organised.

So now
what happens?

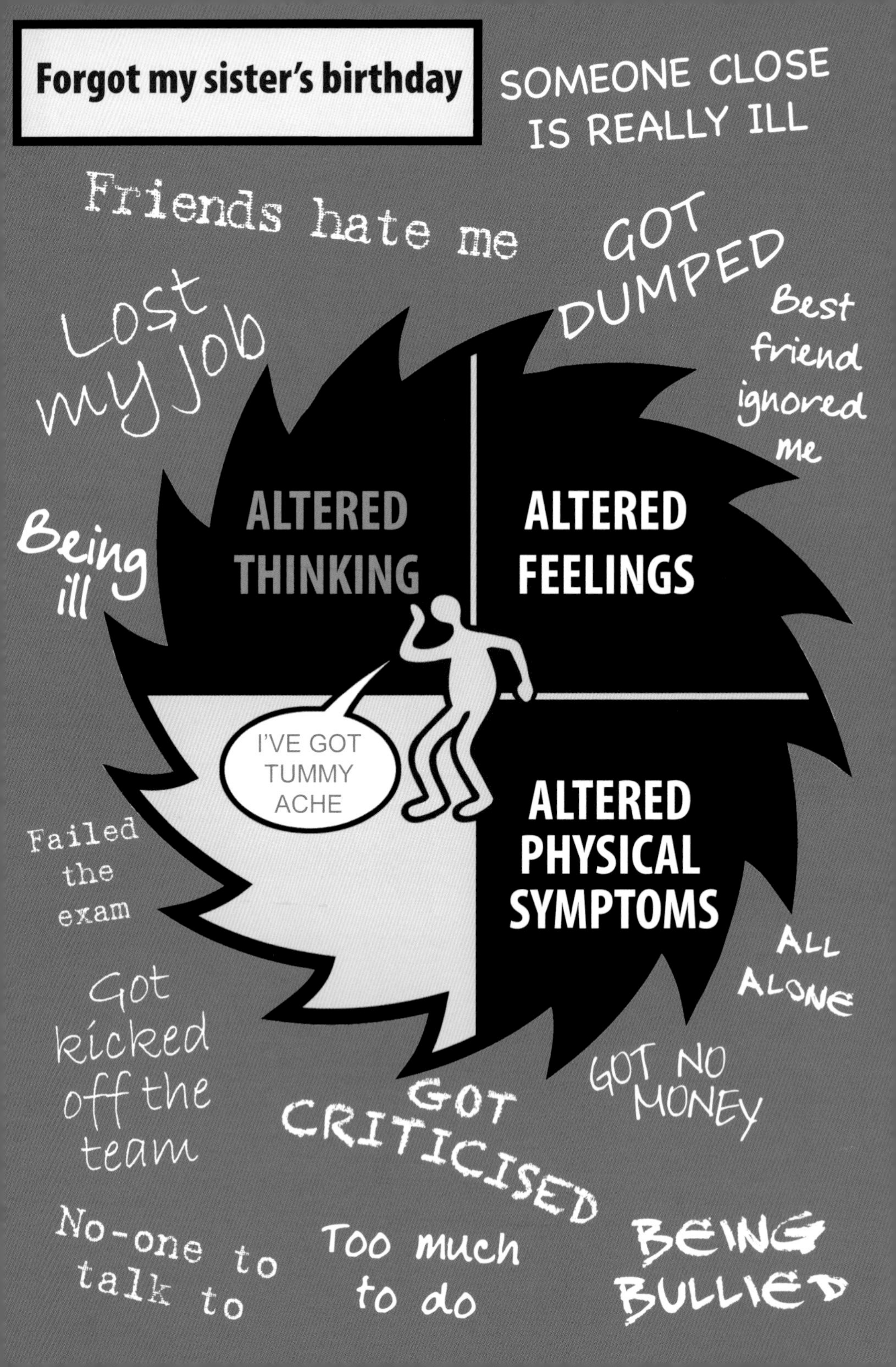

Altered feelings lead to altered physical symptoms

When you feel low or guilty, you can get sweaty and tense and your stomach or your head can ache. Sometimes you can feel really tired.

Your hands might feel clammy, or you feel really tense and can't sit still.

Ever had a sinking feeling or felt your heart racing? It's probably that old vicious cycle spinning round!

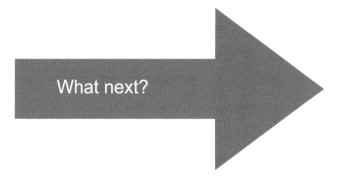

What next?

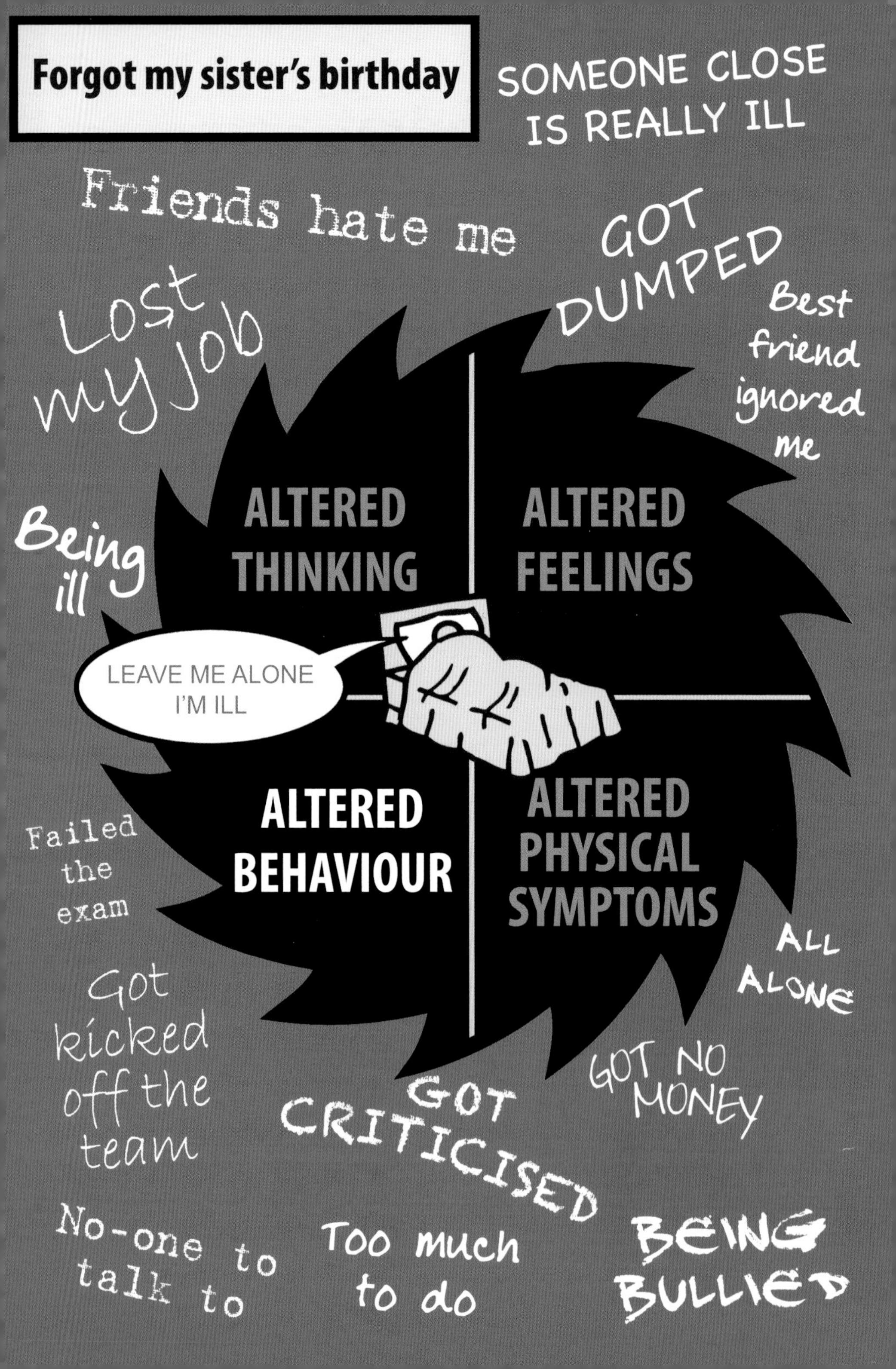

Altered physical symptoms lead to altered behaviour

It's only natural. You're really tired, you have a headache or maybe feel tense, so you don't feel like going out, or even getting up. You steer clear of people who might ask if you sent a card or present. You stay in and hardly do any exercise. You're not eating right and you seem to catch all the bugs that are going round.

You even finish up at the doctor's, asking why you can't seem to shake off this virus you've had for weeks.

And you know what happens then? The cycle goes round again, only this time, you're already ill, staying in bed and fed up, so you get even worse.

Vicious, these cycles, aren't they? That's why it's important to work out how these five areas of life (outside events, thinking, feelings, physical symptoms and behaviour) are affected by how you feel.

Now what about you?

COMPLETE YOUR OWN FIVE AREAS ASSESSMENT

You've read about how you might react if you missed your sister's birthday. Do you fall into other vicious cycles from time to time?

Here's how to play detective and work out how the vicious cycle affects you.

Choose a recent time when you felt bad. To start with, don't pick a time that is really upsetting or distressing. Instead choose a situation when you felt a bit down, fed up, angry, stressed, scared, frustrated, guilty, ashamed, tired, or in pain.

Now use the next two pages to work out how you reacted.

Pen at the ready?

Now's time to spot that vicious cycle!

MY FIVE AREAS ASSESSMENT

Describe the situation:

My thoughts:

Altered
Thinking

Altered
Behaviour

My behaviour:

Altered Feelings

My feelings:

Altered Physical Feelings

My body:

YOUR VICIOUS CYCLE

Did you fall into a vicious cycle?

If you felt bad, it's likely the vicious cycle was spinning. What was the outside event - like a person or difficult situation? Did what you think affect how you felt – in your feelings and physical feelings? How did this affect what you did?

Did anything look familiar? Patterns of thinking, feeling or body reactions often repeat again and again. Did the cycle start to spin and make you feel even worse?

Stopping your cycle spinning takes practise. If you're feeling worse than usual it can feel hard to break the cycle.

Now for the *good* news!

YOU CAN STOP IT SPINNING!

You know the great thing about cycles?
They turn both ways!

In the same way that just one thing (an
altered thought) led to everything else
getting worse, you can start to make it
better by changing one thing.

Just by acting differently, or changing the
way you think about some things, you can
affect all the other things in the cycle and
start to feel better.

Sounds too easy? Turn over for an
example.

How to stop the cycle

1. You're walking down the street and someone you know ignores you

Oh no! She doesn't like me!

4. You have no energy and maybe can't sleep that night for worrying about what happened – altered physical symptoms

Oh no! She doesn't like me!

I feel down

What's wrong with me? I feel tired and exhausted

I don't want to see anyone at the moment

Now lets stop the cycle!

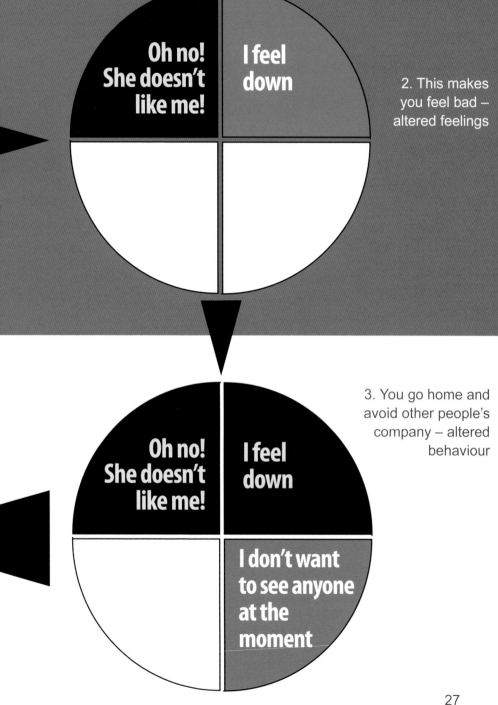

2. This makes you feel bad – altered feelings

3. You go home and avoid other people's company – altered behaviour

27

Start here

1. You're walking down the street and someone you know ignores you

Poor Louise, she must be upset, I wonder what's wrong?

4. You arrange to see Louise later and discuss practical things you can do to help

Poor Louise, she must be upset, I wonder what's wrong?

Is there anything I can do?

I feel really great, alert and strong

I feel good about myself because I'm helping someone else

See how it works?

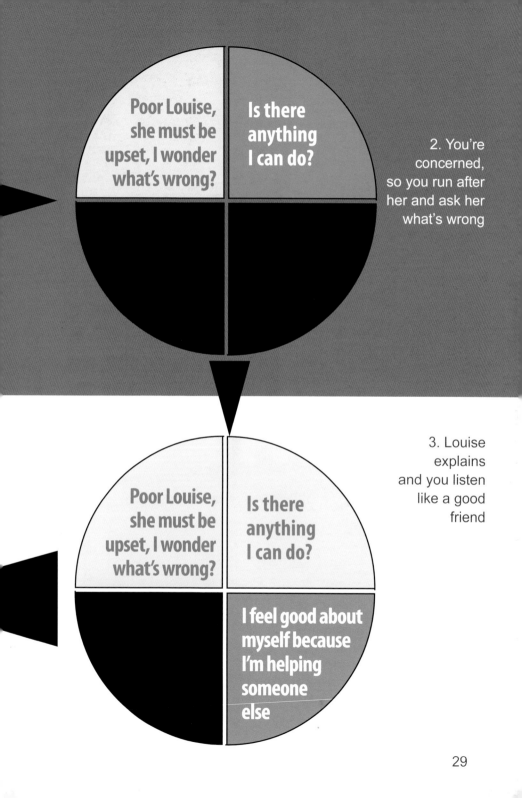

2. You're concerned, so you run after her and ask her what's wrong

3. Louise explains and you listen like a good friend

YOU
HAVE
CONTROL

You just need to change one thing

You can take control and stop the vicious cycle by changing just one thing – your thinking, your response, your activities – almost anything. And it doesn't have to be a big thing!

You could start by changing the way you react. By going out just one time. By doing just a bit more exercise. By changing the way you think about things.

If you manage to do something about just one thing, you'll break the vicious cycle, stop it spinning down and down and start to feel better straight away.

So here's what to do. Pick one small thing then use the Planner sheet on pages 32/33 to give yourself the best start.

Once you're done, use the Review sheet on pages 34/35 to check your progress.

Go, make a plan

Don't just sit there, make a plan!

Planner sheet

1. What am I going to do?

2. When am I going to do it?

3. What problems or difficulties could arise, and how can I overcome them?

Is my planned task -

	Yes	No
Q. Useful for improving my well-being?	☐	☐
Q. Specific, so that I will know when I have done it?	☐	☐
Q. Realistic, practical and achievable?	☐	☐

How did it go?

Review Sheet

What did you plan to do? Write it here:

If yes:

1. What went well?

2. What didn't go so well?

3. What have you learned from what happened?

4. How are you going to apply what you have learned?

Did you try to do it?

Yes   **No**

[ ]   [ ]

If no: what stopped you?

Internal things (forgot, not enough time, put it off, didn't think I could do it, couldn't see the point etc.).

External things (other people, work or home issues etc.).

How can you tackle things differently next time?

NEXT
STEPS

Use the five areas vicious cycle to make sense of why you feel the way you do. Remember, that's not all you've discovered. You've also learned some targets for change that will make a big difference.

What changes do you need to make in each of the five areas? When you've sorted your current problem, you might want to choose another chapter and work on something else in your life.

You can get added help and support by working through the free linked online courses at www.llttf.com.

Go for it!

Introduction to Chapter 2

Do you ever wake up in the morning and think - *"I just can't be bothered doing anything!"* You feel tried and not really wanting to do much at all. That feeling goes away when we get a few good night's sleep or when we slowly come around as the day continues. But what if that feeling sticks around far longer?

Have you ever noticed that if you want some help with something, sometimes someone who is busy responds a lot faster than someone who has little on? That busy person somehow seems to have more energy and focus- and can get things done. In contrast, the person who has less on their plate might put things off and say they'll help later. There's an important truth here - that the less we do, the less likely we are to do anything.

That's important because if we hit a rough patch and start to feel stressed, hassled or down, it can be so easy to feel overwhelmed and start to do less and less. We can withdraw from others, or take to our beds for longer. And a cycle can be set up where the less we do, the worse we feel, and the worse we feel, the less we do.

That's what this chapter focuses on. It will help you discover how you can improve how you feel by choosing to change what you do. It identifies the key ingredients for feeling good – having a daily routine that balances the *should* stuff and the *good* stuff. It helps you identify those good activities- the things you can do that will make you feel better.

Don't forget, you're in control.

Chapter 2

DOING THINGS THAT MAKE YOU FEEL BETTER

(I can't be bothered doing anything)

I feel too ill to do things

It's such a relief staying inside

I FEEL TIRED ALL THE TIME

I hardly see anyone these days

I don't even listen to music anymore

I DO WHAT I HAVE TO DO AND NO MORE

It's all too much effort

I haven't even got the energy to read this book

I do things for everyone else but there's never any time for me

Know what? You're in a vicious cycle

When you feel low, you tend to stop doing things. You don't go out so much, you avoid seeing friends and you even stop listening to music or watching sport.

As a result, you feel even lower, and then you feel like doing even less. It can seem such a relief to cut down and withdraw. It's tempting to take to bed, or sit or lie around all day. But if you do, you end up all seized up, feeling stiff, tired and overwhelmed.

It's like: the less you do, the worse you feel, the worse you feel, the less you do. And it keeps going round and round and round…

Things can get quite vicious.

So, what's going on?

1 **Symptoms make things hard.**
Low, not sleeping/tired.
Scared, fed up.
Can't be bothered.

4 **Count the cost.**
Feel worse, lose confidence.
Less pleasure, less
achievement, see friends less.
You feel worse and worse.

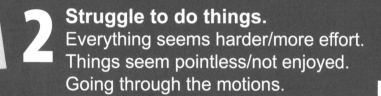

2 **Struggle to do things.**
Everything seems harder/more effort.
Things seem pointless/not enjoyed.
Going through the motions.

3 **It's such a relief to cut
down/avoid things that
seem too hard.**
Do less and less.
Only do things you must/
should do.
"You" time squeezed out.

Turn over to break the cycle

DO YOU KNOW WHAT YOU JUST DID?

You broke the cycle

All it took was a little bit of positive action - turning that page in this case.

Now all you have to do is take another tiny step, then another and another.

What steps? That's what this chapter is about – to show you the easy steps you can take to break that cycle into bits and start feeling better.

It involves making choices. Choosing to do things that make you feel better, rather than hiding away feeling worse and worse.

Important question coming up

WHAT DOES YOUR DAY LOOK LIKE?

When things seem hard, it's easy to lose your previous routine. It's tempting to lie in bed longer, stay up later, or have a longer nap each afternoon. But before you know it you lose the pattern and structure of your day.

What times do you typically get up?

... and go to bed?

These are the anchors that start and end your day. Other anchors that split your day are mealtimes. So, when do you eat?

Breakfast

Lunch

Tea/dinner

Around these points are all the other activities of the day. Meeting friends, household chores and more.
You need to get a routine going again. And start building in activities that you know are good for you.

First, look at what you do just now

Think about yesterday

Start by thinking about the last 24 hours.
Write down everything you have done.
Include things like getting dressed, talking
to a friend on the phone, washing your hair,
etc. Then score them out of ten for
pleasure, achievement and feeling close to
other people. The first few spaces are filled
in to show you how to do it.
Doing this will help you understand what's
good in your life and also to realise what's
missing.

About closeness

Feeling close to others is really important,
but when we're down, we sometimes hide
away. If your diary doesn't have enough
things with a good closeness score, this
chapter will help you sort that out.

	Pleasure	Achievement	Closeness to others
Talking to Sarah on the phone.	9	3	10
Cleaning my room.	1	10	0

Check your list and pick out the things you did that scored highly for pleasure, achievement or closeness to others. Write them down here.

ANYTHING MISSING FROM YOUR DAY?

What about things you've stopped doing?

Your day might not have contained all the things you like to do, so have a look through the list below and tick the one's that apply to you. Things you used to enjoy but haven't felt like doing lately.

Pleasure
- ☐ Enjoying sport.
- ☐ Listening to music.
- ☐ Watching a film.
- ☐ Going for a walk/Getting some fresh air.
- ☐ Playing a musical instrument.
- ☐ Reading a good book, magazine or blog.
- ☐ Practicing relaxation techniques.
- ☐ Cooking or baking for pleasure.

Achievement
- ☐ Pursuing a hobby.
- ☐ Gardening/looking after plants.
- ☐ Doing exercise.
- ☐ Doing drama.

Closeness
- ☐ Seeing your friends.
- ☐ Watching TV with a friend .
- ☐ Phoning or texting friends.
- ☐ Going to a class or club.
- ☐ Going to church, mosque, temple or synagogue.
- ☐ Spending time with family.
- ☐ Helping other people.

Well ticked!

Now choose an activity you want to do

USE WHAT YOU'VE FOUND TO START FILLING YOUR DAY WITH GOOD STUFF

Remember, the things that make you smile.

One of the reasons we feel worse when we stop doing things, is the fact that it's usually the things we like that we avoid first.
No wonder life seems to go down and down!

To start it going up again, you need to pick good things to fill your day with. Not all the time – just one thing to start with. So the next step of your plan is to look at the lists you just made and pick one of the things on them.

Pick something that used to give you pleasure, or a sense of achievement. Or something that you think is worthwhile or made you feel close to others.

Just one thing to start with.

An activity you value and see as important to your life.

NOW WRITE
IT HERE
SO YOU DON'T
FORGET IT.

_____

_____

_____

_____

GOOD

You've just written down the thing you're going to start doing again. Something worth getting up for.

Now, you're going to do it

NOW PLAN WHEN YOU'LL DO IT

Say what and when

Think about the activity you want to do first.

Write down *what* you will do, and *when* you will do it into the Activity Planner on the next two pages.

Just now it will stand out as the only activity there.

Go, ahead, write it in.

You don't want it to feel lonely, so soon you'll be adding other activities into the Activity Planner.

But to start with just include:
- The single activity you planned - the one you wrote down on page 53.
- Next, add your daily anchors: the meals you have through the day, and the times you get up and go to bed.

There's plenty of time to add more activities, but for now just focus on the first activity you're going to do.

My activity planner

Plan a balance of activities over the days and week.

Get into a routine- a time to get up, eat, go to bed, and do the household chores, or perhaps to go for a walk, meet friends or attend a regular class.

Choose things you Value and give a sense of Pleasure, Achievement or Closeness to others.

Plan in the key essentials that otherwise will build up and cause you problems- paying bills, cutting the lawn, doing the washing up, ironing, having a hair cut etc.

The plan is to build what you do up over a few weeks so you end up with one activity planned in each part of the day. Leave some gaps for the unexpected things that crop up. Have some time just for you.

linked
worksheet
www.llttf.com

	Morning	Afternoon	Evening
Monday			
Tuesday			
Wednesday			
Thursday			
Friday			
Saturday			
Sunday			

Now build on it

REMEMBER THAT LONELY ACTIVITY?

Now let's give it some friends

Add some more regular activities

Having to get out of bed to walk the dog or feed the baby can be a real pain, especially on cold mornings, but it's also a great way to feel better. No dog? No baby? Then make yourself a routine with other things. Shaving and showering. Cleaning the house. Popping to the corner shop to say hello and buy some bread and eggs. Cooking them for breakfast! Can't get out? Make the most of activities you can do.

And if you rebuild your routine with things that involve others (ringing your mum each morning, walking with a friend every Wednesday) you'll feel even better because of that closeness thing we mentioned before.

It needs to be a daily routine, too. Choose something every single day that you need to get up and out of bed for. Don't lie in - remember, the less you do the worse you feel, the worse you feel, the less you do. Add these to your Activity Planner.

More good stuff on the next page

ADD SOME MORE OF THE GOOD STUFF

Plan a series of other activities, then add them one by one into your Activity Planner. Make each activity small and not scary. Don't be ambitious, be easy on yourself. And don't worry if you have to keep crossing things out, there's plenty of space.

- Choose some of the good stuff that helps how you feel.

- Add in some of the things you've cut down or stopped doing that used to be good too.

- Choose things you value and give a sense of pleasure, achievement or closeness.

- Build things up over a few weeks so you end up with one activity planned in each part of the day.

With each activity you add, you're breaking that vicious cycle, and making it spin the other way so you feel better and better.

Are you ignoring important things?

Some activities may seem hard or boring. Paying the bills, looking after yourself, keeping up with the housework - they can all seem too much trouble when you're feeling down.

The problem is some activities are necessary, and if you don't do them it makes you feel worse and can get you in a mess. So here's what to do: choose one thing that wasn't in your diary but should have been, and plan to do it - now.

Pay that bill. Make that call. Get your hair done. Do some tidying. Wash the dishes.

You'll feel loads better afterwards and you'll be able to add it to your diary and put a 10 in the 'achievement' box!

Aim for the following

You know what makes you feel good.

Across each day and week you need to get a mix of activities that help.

Start with the activities you can change most easily.
Aim for variety so you address each of the key areas:

1. Pleasure: things that make you feel good.
2. Achievement: things you value and see as important.
3. Closeness: where you connect with important others.
4. Finally don't forget to do things that are important and necessary.

Each of these activities breaks the vicious cycle and makes you feel better.
But don't rush. Some activities need to be built up to slowly.

TAKING STEPS THAT MOVE YOU FORWARDS

Some activities may be good for you, but seem just too hard to do all at once. You need to work up to doing them step by step.

How?

Have a look at the example opposite.

For example

Jack used to like meeting his friends for a walk in the park, but since he's been low, he hasn't had the energy for it. This is what he wrote in his plan for getting back to meeting them.

Step 1. Go to the park and just sit there enjoying the peace and quiet.

Step 2. Go back to the park and walk by myself. Don't need to talk to anyone if I don't feel like it.

Step 3. Get into the habit of walking by myself 2 or 3 times a week.

Step 4. Get in touch with one friend and arrange to have a walk and a chat.

Step 5. Go to the park with my friend at a time when we're likely to see the others.

Step 6. Arrange to meet the others next time they're walking in the park.

Step 7. Keep going – get into a routine and feel the difference!

Jack knew he could take one step a day, or one step a week, it didn't matter. What mattered was having a plan and making steady progress towards getting some fun back in his life.

Right, that's enough of Jack. Now back to your plan.

WRITE DOWN AN ACTIVITY THAT YOU NEED TO BUILD UP TO STEP BY STEP HERE

_____

_____

Now think about the little steps you can take towards doing it. Don't be overly ambitious, be easy on yourself. And don't worry if you have to keep crossing things out, there's plenty of space.

1. I'm going to _____

2. Then I'm going to _____

3. Next, I'm going to _____

4. Then I'm going to _____

5. _____

6. _____

7. _____

8. _____

9. _____

10. _____

SOUNDS EASY DOESN'T IT?

But you know change sometimes isn't that easy

Remember all those failed New Year's resolutions? Promises to change that seem hard? Or maybe we forget, or find we can't be bothered, or talk ourselves out of things?

So, let's recognise something. It's hard to make changes. That's why we've asked you to pick activities to do that you know can be good for you.

But if you find you get stuck doing a particular activity, here's a helping hand to make a plan to do it that will work.

Turn over to make your plan.

Make a plan!

Planner Sheet

1. What am I going to do?

2. When am I going to do it?

3. What problems or difficulties could arise, and how can I overcome them?

linked
worksheet
www.llttf.com

Is my planned task -

	Yes	No
Q. Useful for understanding or changing how I am?	☐	☐
Q. Specific, so that I will know when I have done it?	☐	☐
Q. Realistic, practical and achievable?	☐	☐

MY PLAN
1 ___
2 ___
3 ___

HOW
DID
IT GO?

Life's all about learning

If you make a plan and everything goes smoothly- that's great!

But you can also learn a lot from when things go wrong too. So, if there are problems with your plan- that's great too. It's great because you can play detective and learn.

So, if you got stuck, or something was difficult, ask yourself some questions. Was the problem something *internal* – inside you, or *external* – for example a problem caused by someone else, the weather, or unexpected circumstances?

Use whatever you discover to make your next plan even better.

You'll find a useful Review sheet to help you with this learning on the next two pages.

Try to get into a sequence of *Plan* (using the Planner sheet), *Do*, and *Review* (using the Review sheet) for whenever you are planning more difficult activities. That way you will keep moving forwards.

How did it go?

Review Sheet

What did you plan to do? Write it here:

If yes:

1. What went well?

2. What didn't go so well?

3. What have you learned from what happened?

4. How are you going to apply what you have learned?

linked
worksheet
www.llttf.com

Review
Day

Did you try to do it?

Yes   **No**

☐   ☐

If no: what stopped you?

Internal things (forgot, not enough time, put it off, didn't think I could do it, couldn't see the point etc.).

External things (other people, work or home issues etc.).

How can you tackle things differently next time?

WHAT IF SOMETHING GOT IN YOUR WAY?

Learn from it. So as soon as you've written your next plan, think about what could stop it happening. Are there things that might trip you up? What about other people? Could someone be unhelpful at any stage?

When you've figured out what could block your progress, work out another mini-plan for getting around the obstacle. It's called unblocking.

Things to watch out for

Don't try and make every change possible all at once.

Be realistic – you're planning for success not a let-down. You know your own personality and how inpatient or ambitious you are. That's where it's important to be wise and plan just one main change a day to start with.

So, pick just a few things to get you started, and make a separate plan to do each using the Planner sheet. Then plan them in across the day and the week using the Activity Planner.

1. Leave some gaps for the unexpected things that crop up.
2. Include some time just for you.
3. Remember the anchors - a time to get up, eat, go to bed.
4. Add in some more routines like a regular time to do the household chores, or perhaps to go for a walk, meet friends or attend a regular class.
5. Make sure your plan fits with your values/ideals of how you want to live.

But don't forget that some things are important to do even if they aren't much fun or seem difficult.

AT THE END OF EACH DAY

Use your Happy List to help you remember

Each evening, sit down and write down three things that you:

- Have enjoyed.
- Felt was a job well done.
- Or helped you feel close to someone else.

What are you thankful for?

After a few days, you'll have a list of great things that you can look back on. It will help you remember how you're changing things.

Time to give yourself a pat on the back!

Now, keep going with more plans until you get a good balance of activities across the day and the week. You'll feel the difference!

Go for it!

Introduction to Chapter 3

Have you ever looked through a Kaleidoscope? Everything seems beautiful and colourful. The red, green, yellow and blue shapes form in fantastic combinations and draw your attention.

How we think can be like that. We can choose to focus on the amazing, the good things, the people around us we like and who like us, the places we love and the hobbies and interests we enjoy.

But sometimes it can seem the opposite happens. We become focused on the difficulties - the challenges and the hard things in life. We may notice the things we haven't done more than the things we have done. We pick over our faults and weaknesses rather than celebrate the good things in our lives.

In this chapter you'll discover what Bad thoughts are and what they look like. Bad thoughts are thoughts that make us feel worse, in our feelings, bodies or relationships. Like celebrities they crave attention and always like to be in the spotlight. But maybe not everything they say is always true, helpful or accurate.

At times when we feel under pressure Bad thoughts pop into our minds more, and are harder to shift. They become a focus and start to make us feel even more stressed, down or emotional. Together they also cause us to react in ways that make things worse such as withdrawing from others, or doing things that can backfire on how we feel.

You'll learn some effective ways of relating differently to these upsetting bad thoughts. This chapter will help you play detective, spot the bad thoughts and put them in their place.

Remember, you have control.

Chapter 3

LOOKING AT THINGS DIFFERENTLY

(Why does everything always go wrong?)

Everyone thinks I'm a loser

Nobody likes me

I ALWAYS MESS UP

IF I DON'T GET THIS SORTED OUT – I WON'T COPE

WHAT'S THE POINT

THINGS NEVER WORK OUT FOR ME

It's all my fault

Sound familiar?

That's because loads of people think that way - but when you're already feeling pretty bad, thoughts like these make you feel even worse.

Bad thoughts are called that because they can have a damaging impact on how we feel and what we do.

This chapter will show you how.

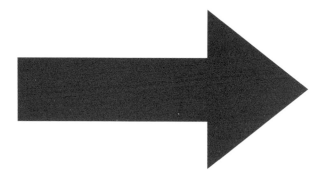

Turn the page and you'll see what we mean.

GOOD MOVE!

You turned the page!

You didn't say "Oh, forget it!" and chuck the book out of the window. You turned the page and took a giant leap towards feeling better - by yourself.

Keep on turning and you'll find out how to *keep on* feeling better and better, with the

AMAZING BAD-THOUGHT-BUSTING PROGRAMME

Now you're going to learn to spot some bad thoughts.

LET'S PLAY DETECTIVE

Magnifying Glass at the ready?

The key to good detective work is to slow things down and be on the lookout.

Try this task to start noticing your own bad thoughts.

Imagine yourself into each situation, and try to spot the thoughts that pop into your mind.

1). You're late for an important meeting. You're stuck in traffic and can see the building you want to reach. You know you're going to be really late.

2). You invite friends round for a meal, but notice one of them doesn't eat much of it and says they're not hungry.

3). You play sport but this week you're not picked to play.

Then complete the worksheet on pages 88-89. Use the questions to help you identify the thoughts that occur. Write down as many as you notice, then turn the page to label the thoughts.

My Bad Thoughts

How to fill in this sheet

Think about the difficult situation.

What went through your mind?

- About you?
- About others?
- About what has happened?
- About what might happen?
- About what others think about you?

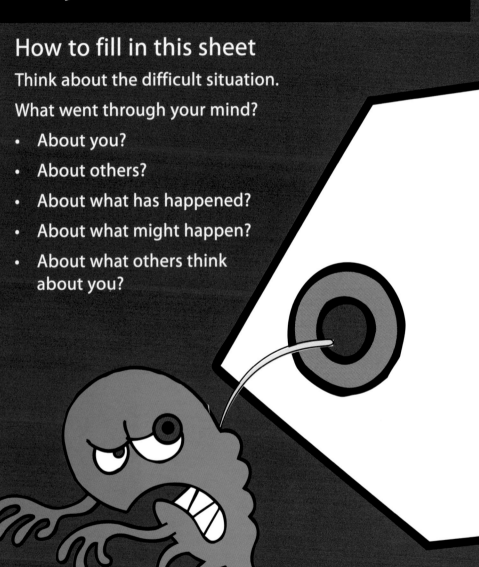

linked
worksheet
www.llttf.com

BAD THOUGHT SPOTTER

Bad thoughts are also known as unhelpful thinking styles. They are habits of thinking we can fall into time and time again. These thoughts need tackling because:

- they worsen how we feel emotionally and physically
- they affect what we do. So, we might say no to something when yes could be fun.

This bad thought spotter will help you spot when your thinking isn't helping.

Look back at the thoughts you wrote down on the last two pages. Now label them using the bad thought spotter on page 91.

Are any of these thinking styles familiar? Have you been here before?

If you tick one or more boxes on the right, you've spotted a bad thought that you can fix with the Amazing Bad Thought Busting Programme.

UNHELPFUL THINKING STYLES	Tick
Are you your own worst critic? Do you always seem to be beating yourself up about something?	
Do you focus on the bad stuff? As if you were looking at the world through darkened glasses?	
Do you have a gloomy view of the future? Expecting everything to turn out badly.	
Are you jumping to the worst conclusions? It's called 'catastrophising'.	
Do you assume that others see you badly? When you haven't checked whether it's true, it's called 'Mind-reading'.	
Do you take responsibility for everything? Including things that aren't your fault.	
Are you always saying things like 'Should' 'Ought to' 'Got to'? Setting impossible standards for yourself?	

Turn the page to beat these bad thoughts

First, label the thought

When you notice one of your bad thoughts, don't get caught up in it, just mentally step back and stick a label on it.

"Oh that's just one of those bad thoughts".

When you label a bad thought this way, **it** loses its power and **you** realise it's just part of being upset.

It's not the truth, it's just one of those bad thoughts.

You could even talk to it. Say: "You're spotted! I'm not playing that game again!"

Turn over for **STEP 2**

NOW LEAVE IT ALONE

Mentally turn your back on the bad thought. Don't challenge it or try to argue with it, just let it be.

Bad thoughts love attention so don't give them any.

Instead, think about what you're doing right now, or stuff that you're planning for the future, or things you've achieved lately.

STEP 3 next

STAND UP TO IT!

Don't be bossed about by bad thoughts

Bad thoughts are like bullies - they can be intimidating. But although they sound strong, really they're weak underneath. And they tell lies.

They say you won't like doing something. They say you'll fail if you try. They tell you you're rubbish or you're scared or nobody likes you.
But this is just the bad thought,not the truth.
Don't be bullied!
If the thought says "Don't" then DO!
If the thought says "Can't" say "CAN!"
Right back at it.

Easy for us to say? You're right.

But if you don't give it a try you'll never know. And, just what if you really did beat those bad thoughts?

Turn over for the next step

GIVE YOURSELF A BREAK

Be a better friend to yourself, you deserve it.

Bad thoughts are how we beat ourselves up when we're upset. We often say things to ourselves that are critical and nasty – things we would never say to someone we cared for. And we often say things to ourselves in such a nasty or scary tone.

So if you're having trouble with a bad thought, think what a person who really loved and wanted the best for you would say. What words of encouragement and support might they offer?

They'd disagree with the bad thoughts. They'd remind you that you're not rubbish, or stupid, or bound to fail.

Trust these compassionate things and let them help you get rid of the bad thoughts.

Turn over for **STEP 5**

99

HOW TO BEAT THE REALLY BAD ONES

Some bad thoughts are hard to beat.

They keep coming back and you wonder if you'll ever get the better of them.

Here are three things you can do that will help.

Look at the situation differently

First, imagine what it would be like if it was a friend, not you, who was having this bad thought. What advice would you give? Now give the same advice to yourself.

Put your thought or worry into perspective. Will it matter in six months? Will you even remember what the problem was? If it won't matter in six months, it's probably not that important now.

How would others deal with the problem? Think about someone who seems to handle problems well and work out what they would do, or how they would think in this situation.

Really Bad Thought

Turn over to **RECAP**

101

SO:

THE AMAZING BAD-THOUGHT-BUSTING PROGRAMME

Bad thoughts mess you up and actually **cause** bad feelings. Beat bad thoughts and you'll feel better. When you notice a bad thought:

1. LABEL IT
Oh, you're just one of those bad thoughts.

2. LEAVE IT
A bad thought needs attention, so don't give it any.

3. STAND UP TO IT
Bad thoughts can be scary but like bullies are weak underneath, and they tell lies. You can beat them.

4. GIVE YOURSELF A BREAK
What would someone who really loved you say? Trust them and let them help you beat the bad thought.

5. LOOK AT IT DIFFERENTLY
Give yourself the advice you'd give to a friend. Ask yourself if it will matter in six months. Pick someone you know and work out how they would handle the situation.

So what are you waiting for? Let's try it out

The Amazing Bad-thought-busting Programme

SHEET 1

1. Label it

Oh, you're just one of those bad thoughts.

2. Leave it

A bad thought needs attention, so don't give it any.

3. Stand up to it

Bad thoughts are like bullies - weak underneath. You can beat them.

TM

4. Give yourself a break

What would someone who really loved you say? Trust them and let them help you beat the bad thought.

5. Look at it differently

- Give yourself the advice you'd give a friend.
- Ask yourself if it will matter in six months.
- Pick someone you know and work out how they would handle the situation.
- Ask yourself if it matters so much.
- Are you basing this on how you feel rather than the facts?
- What would other people say?
- Are you looking at the whole picture?

linked worksheet www.llttf.com

TM

GO
FOR
IT!

Don't worry

If this seems hard at first. A good place to start is to practice on bad thoughts that are only slightly upsetting to begin with.

It takes practice to beat bad thoughts.

But the Amazing Bad Thought Busting Programme really works, so keep trying and within a few days, you'll have your bad thoughts on the run and be feeling better.

Remember the key things is to plan to practice this approach.

Go for it!

Don't just sit there, make a plan!

Planner sheet

1. What am I going to do?

2. When am I going to do it?

3. What problems or difficulties could arise, and how can I overcome them?

Is my planned task -

	Yes	No
Q. Useful for improving my well-being?	☐	☐
Q. Specific, so that I will know when I have done it?	☐	☐
Q. Realistic, practical and achievable?	☐	☐

Introduction to Chapter 4

Can you think of someone you know who is really confident? It might be someone on television, or in a band? Or maybe a footballer or sports personality? What is it about them that makes them stand out as confident?

Is it how they stand? What they say or how they say it? Or is their confidence communicated through their clothes, hair or life style? Many young people look up to people like that, admire them and want to be more like them. The key in growing up isn't to try and act and be like someone else. Instead, it's to let the real you come out.

This chapter will help you discover the origins of confidence. The things that have been said to you that have encouraged you and given you confidence, or have drained confidence and left you with doubts. The good news is that we're learning new things all the time, and that can be true of confidence also. So, you just need to learn to trust and remind yourself of the many things that make you an OK person. You don't have to be a star to shine and be comfortable in yourself.

You will learn some positive things to remind yourself of whenever you feel small. You'll also get to practice some skills that will build your confidence to express yourself and present yourself well.

Finally, you'll also learn about the advantages and disadvantages of having high standards. High standards can push people to achieve good things. However high standards can also bring consequences. It can be stressful trying to live up to such standards, especially if you're struggling just now and feel under pressure. Instead, you'll learn that good enough is good enough.

You have the power to choose.

Chapter 4

BUILDING INNER CONFIDENCE

(I'm not good enough)

I JUST CANT DO IT

I don't fit in

I'm boring

People don't like me

I'm not good looking

I'm not like everyone else

I MESS EVERYTHING UP

I don't like me

I keep making mistakes

Who says you're not good enough?

You weren't born thinking 'I'm not good enough'. Someone or something made you feel that way, perhaps a long time ago.

Maybe your parents didn't praise you or show that they cared enough when you were young, or maybe you weren't around them enough to pick up their real thoughts because they were out working or away a lot of the time. Maybe your classmates were cruel about your shape, size or abilities. Maybe you expect so much of yourself that 'failure' is bound to happen.

Whichever way the idea got into your head, the fact is it's there now, and it's been rattling around for so long that you believe it.

When you believe you're no good, you start to behave as if it's true – hiding away, not trying new things, keeping quiet about what you want, apologising all the time, not bothering to look after yourself. All of which means you don't live or enjoy your life as much as you could.

But you can change. This chapter contains an easy plan for replacing bad ideas (like 'I'm no good') with much more sensible ones (like 'I'm alright really').

Turn the page and
see what happens

WELL DONE!

You chose to make a change

Keep doing that and your problems will soon be over.

How come? Well because it's so easy to believe ideas like "I'm useless"or "I'll never change". But these are just ideas that got in your head a while ago. If a different idea had got in there instead, like "I'm alright really", you wouldn't be reading this chapter.

So what we're going to do in the next few pages is show you how to develop positive ideas about yourself, and put them into your head, where they should have been all along.

Then, when you have a choice of things to believe, you can pick the right one, like you did a minute ago.

Sounds simple, doesn't it? So what are you going to do?

Keep reading - because change occurs step by step

YOU'RE GETTING GOOD AT THIS

So let's get some positive ideas going

If we told you the earth is flat, you wouldn't believe us, because you've been abroad and didn't drop off the edge. You have the evidence.

It's the same with ideas about yourself. It's hard to believe "I'm alright really" when you don't think you've got any evidence for it. So the first step in your plan is to spot some OK things about yourself and write them down.

Things you did well. Times you were helpful to others. Times you did something even when it was hard. Things you do that people thank you for. Things you know a lot about. Things you can do easily or quickly. Times when you make a good contribution to a group activity. People who like you… like that.

Turn over and list some OK things about yourself

Well done!

You turned to the OK Things list! It may take a while to come up with good stuff, because you've lost the habit of thinking you're OK. You are, though, so get writing!

Things I like about me

* Remember, we're looking for things you did well, times when you were helpful to others, people who like you and so on.

NOW LEARN YOUR LIST BY HEART

And say it to yourself whenever you feel small

You now have a list of reasons to believe you're OK, and every one is real and true, unlike those "I'm no good" ideas that sometimes come into your head.

Learn the list, and add more things to it as you think of them.

Keep repeating it so that it really sticks in your mind. Say it to yourself before going to sleep. Recite it quietly when you have a moment to yourself.

After a while, it will help to replace some of the negative ideas that have been hanging around for so long.

I'M OK
I'M OK

Even better, you can also use your list in emergencies, whenever you get into a situation that makes you feel small.

Just read the list over and over again and it will start to change the other stuff. It's just like you did on the last few pages, choosing a more sensible option instead of the "I'm useless" one.

Over the page is a summary that could help you even more.

Turn over for more help

DON'T THINK THIS

I can't do it

I'm not good looking

I'm boring

People don't like me

I'm not good at things

I mess everything up

THINK THIS

I can do it because I did
(something from your list)

I look just fine

I'm interesting, I know about
(something from your list)

Some people like me, including
(some people from your list)

I have strengths and weaknesses like everyone does

I'm good at
(something from your list)

So you know how to
~~change how you think~~

What's next?

CHANGE WHAT YOU DO

How to build your confidence step by step

Everyone has an inside and an outside, and they're different.

You know those people who seem so confident? They're just like you inside, but they know a trick – walk confident, talk confident and you *become* confident.

So what you need to do is be yourself and make some small, steady changes to let the real you shine.

To begin with, take a good look at how you present to others. Think about:

1. What you wear.
2. How you stand.
3. What you say, and how you say it.

You'll also need to become very observant.

Now you get to make some changes

STEPS TO IMPROVING YOUR CONFIDENCE

How do other people do it?

Watch the way confident people stand. It's straight, isn't it? They often seem a bit taller than they really are.

Now pay attention to the way they hold themselves and move. There's no shuffling about, no slumping in chairs, no hiding in corners. And when they're speaking to you, they look you directly in the eye.

Now listen to the way they speak. They're pretty loud, aren't they? And they often speak quite slowly, not having to rush because they somehow know that everyone will keep on listening.

Your task is to slowly work towards this so people see the real you.

Remember, most confident people aren't like that all the way through, they just know how to act confident on the outside, which is what you'll be doing.

After a while you'll start to notice a real difference in how you present yourself.

Turn over for more helpful hints

DON'T DO THIS

Mumble

Talk too quickly

Slump in your chair

Hunch over

Look away or look down

Shut down conversations

DO
THIS

Try to speak a little louder and clearer

Slow down and pause while speaking

Sit up straight, shoulders back

Walk tall, lift your chin up

Make eye contact with others as much as possible, and smile

Ask questions to get conversations going

AM I UP TO THIS?

Yes, you are!

It sounds like a lot to do, doesn't it?
To change your thinking and then start
practising ways to become a more
confident you.

But you only have to do these things a little
bit at first. Make that list of things you like
about yourself, and just try reciting it once or
twice, when you feel small. Pick a confident
person and notice one of their mannerisms
to start with.

You won't become the life and soul of the
party overnight and you might not even
want to be that loud and bouncy anyway.

You're not here to become a big pop star or
a famous actor.

It's more about finding new ways to act
confident, but do it in your own style.

This way to a very
important thing

GOOD ENOUGH IS GOOD ENOUGH

Don't beat yourself up

In the real world, you don't have to get straight A's to be happy, successful and popular.

In fact the world's happiest people are those who are content with themselves as they are.

So whenever you're being hard on yourself for not doing something perfectly, not coming top of the class or finishing first in the race, say this to yourself -

There's no such thing as perfect. Just do what you can do.

YOU'RE DOING FINE

Here's how to stay that way

1. Choose sensible ideas not bad ones.
Fill in your list of things you like about you, learn it by heart and use it to change the negative ideas in your head.

Recite it to yourself before going to sleep. Use the list in situations that make you feel small and choose the "I'm OK" idea, not the "I'm useless" one.

2. Walk and talk with confidence.
Remember, most confident people aren't like that all the way through, they just know how to *act* confident on the outside.

So do the same. Walk confident, talk confident, look confident and you'll **be** confident.

3. Remember, there is no such thing as perfect. Just do what you can.
Nobody's perfect, so don't beat yourself up because you can't reach an impossible goal.

So, here's what to do. Pick one small thing, then use the *Planner* sheet on pages 136-137 to give yourself the best start.

Once you're done, use the *Review* sheet on pages 138-139 to check your progress.

Good Luck!

Go for it!

Make a plan!

Planner Sheet

1. What am I going to do?

2. When am I going to do it?

3. What problems or difficulties could arise, and how can I overcome them?

Is my planned task -

Q. Useful for understanding or changing how I am?

Yes ☐ **No** ☐

Q. Specific, so that I will know when I have done it?

Yes ☐ **No** ☐

Q. Realistic, practical and achievable?

Yes ☐ **No** ☐

How did it go?
Review Sheet

What did you plan to do? Write it here:

If yes:

1. What went well?

2. What didn't go so well?

3. What have you learned from what happened?

4. How are you going to apply what you have learned?

Review Day

Did you try to do it?

Yes **No**

If no: what stopped you?

Internal things (forgot, not enough time, put it off, didn't think I could do it, couldn't see the point etc.).

External things (other people, work or home issues etc.).

How can you tackle things differently next time?

Introduction to Chapter 5

Most of us can tackle problems most of the time. But if there are too many challenges that we face all at once, or if the problems seem huge and overwhelming, then most of us can start to feel the pressure and begin to feel out of control.

It's so easy when we feel there's too much being demanded to feel daunted. We look at the amount of work, or the mountain of other demands we face and feel stuck, not knowing how to even start.

There's an added difficulty. At times when we feel stressed or down, we can find it difficult coming up with possible plans to sort out the problem. Even if we can come up with some solutions, if we feel stressed it's more likely we'll dismiss each possible response as not being likely to work.

The result is we feel trapped as if we are in a one way street and can't get out. All we focus on is the problem and our sense of powerlessness. So, what do we need to do? Just like that blind alley or a dead end you need to stop, look around and get clear where you are, then figure out how to plan your way out of there.

In this chapter you will learn an approach that you can use to tackle any problem. Yes, really, any problem. Whether you want to save or make some money, complete a project at home, tackle your neighbour who is playing their music too loud when you're trying to sleep or even learn to play the guitar!

Remember, when it comes to problems, you'll learn a fresh and effective plan you can use.

Chapter 5

HOW TO
FIX
ALMOST
EVERYTHING

IN 4 EASY STEPS

(a guide to practical problem solving)

Finish a project

Lose some weight

GET A JOB

SPEND WISELY

Get fitter

Revise for exams

GET ACTIVE

Make more friends

Plan for a holiday

get out more

Yes, almost everything

It doesn't matter what you want to do, this Easy 4-Step Plan will help you do it.

It works particularly well if you're feeling low. In fact it works even if you're so fed up you can only just be bothered reading this page.

The idea is to break your problem or target into tiny little chunks that, by themselves, are easy to do.

Then you work out how you're going to do each chunk, make a plan, and carry it out. It's called the Easy 4-Step Plan.

It's like eating an elephant

HOW TO EAT AN ELEPHANT

a. Break elephant into small chunks

b. Eat one chunk at a time

If you love elephants (and we do too!) then think instead of how to eat a big pumpkin.

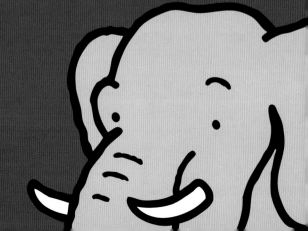

Problems are like elephants

They look huge. Far too big to deal with. But when you break them into smaller bits, they're much less frightening and a lot easier to fix (or eat). That's why step 1 of the E4SP is 'break your problem into pieces'.

Let's say you you feel you never see your friends. You could break the week into bits and make an effort to see them on Mondays, for example.

If you think you are spending too much time alone you could try watching TV with someone a couple of nights a week instead of sitting in your room. Why not phone your friends and have a conversation rather than texting?

Or if you feel you're on social media or watching TV too much, you could start by not doing it for an afternoon or a day. Most tasks can be chopped up like this, and everyone* agrees that you're much more likely to succeed when you do things bit by bit.

*Everyone except elephants.

Turn over for **STEP 2**

TM

BRAINSTORM WAYS TO DO THE FIRST PIECE

Grab a piece of paper...

And write down all the things you could do to work on the first bit of the problem.

The trick with brainstorming is to let your mind run free, and write everything down - the wacky things as well as the sensible ones.

To start seeing more of your friends, you could join an evening class that is held every Monday.

Spending too much time watching TV? You could get out one of those board games you like to play at holiday time. Or ask a friend to play sport. Or choose to chat about people's days as you eat in the evening.

Trying to cut down on social media or apps? Leave your phone in another room. Or put it on silent for part of the day. Switch it off at a certain time in the evening.

If you write everything down, there's bound to be a good idea in there somewhere.

STEP 3 next

CHOOSE AN IDEA AND MAKE A PLAN TO DO IT

Step by step

Look at your brainstorm ideas and pick one. Choose one that looks do-able and doesn't scare you too much.

Now take another piece of paper and write down, step by step, how to actually DO it.

Make the steps as small as you like: Get up. Get dressed. Walk to front door. Open door…. and so on.

OR

To see friends more: text a friend, look at activities you could do together, sign up for an evening class, invite someone to your new favourite coffee shop….like that.

OR

For using social media less: leave your phone in the other room, forget your phone on purpose one day when you go out, set your phone and computer up to block some social media sites. Make sure that the steps are small, straightforward and seem like things you could really do.

What if something gets in the way?

As soon as you've written your plan, think about what could stop it happening. Are there any unforeseen events that might trip you up? What about other people? Could someone be unhelpful at any stage?

When you've figured out what might block your progress, work out another mini-plan for getting round the obstacle.

Final step coming up

This way, you'll be ready for whatever happens!

149

CHECK THE PLAN AND PUT IT INTO ACTION

This is it! You've written down all the steps, now you need to check that they're do-able. Use this checklist:

Is it realistic?
You're not planning to run a marathon are you?

☐

Are you aiming at just one thing?
Don't try and do more than one item on your list. You can always pick another when you've sorted the first one.

☐

Is it slow?
There's no need to rush at things. Your plan can take as long as you like, so long as you stick to it, step by step.

☐

Is it easy?
Make your steps small and easy and you'll be more likely to do them.

☐

Are you ready to unblock it?
Have you thought about what could go wrong and how to deal with it?

☐

✔✔✔✔✔

FIVE TICKS?

THEN GO FOR IT!

Still a bit doubtful?

THAT'S EASY FOR YOU TO SAY!

Don't worry, you can do it.

The Easy 4-Step Plan really works, even when you have a really tough problem to deal with.

Remember the elephant – you can eat it or a large pumpkin piece by piece. All you have to do is keep on eating!

And don't beat yourself up if things go wrong half way through. Just calmly go back to the plan and take those small, steady steps again.

Why not try it now using the next two pages?

MY E4SP

My problem

---

1. Break it into chunks

---

2. Brainstorm ways to do the first piece

linked worksheet www.llttf.com

3. Choose an idea and make a plan to do it

---

4. Check the plan and put it into action

Is it realistic?	✔
Are you aiming at just one thing?	✔
Is it slow?	✔
Is it easy?	✔
Are you ready to unblock it?	✔

TM

NOW DO IT

TRY OUT YOUR PLAN

Moving forward bit by bit

Now you have used the Easy 4-Step Plan to plan the first change, you need to do it. Sounds easy? But we all know sometimes we can get stuck or derailed. We may lose motivation, talk ourselves out of it, or maybe things change and the initial plan needs changing. Or we forget.

That's where making a clear plan to put what you've learned into action can help. The Planner sheet on the next two pages can really help. It helps provide a double check on your plan- and also forces you to be clear exactly what you are going to do and when you are going to do it.

Remember to work on your problem bit by bit using the Easy 4-Step and Planner sheets to plan each step one at a time (remember that poor elephant!).
You can download more worksheets for free from www.llttf.com.

Don't just sit there, make a plan!

Planner sheet

1. What am I going to do?

2. When am I going to do it?

3. What problems or difficulties could arise, and how can I overcome them?

Is my planned task -

Q. Useful for improving
   my well-being?

Yes ☐   No ☐

Q. Specific, so that I will
   know when I have done it?

Yes ☐   No ☐

Q. Realistic, practical
   and achievable?

Yes ☐   No ☐

WHAT TO DO WHEN THE GOING GETS TOUGH

Remind yourself why you're doing this

If you're having trouble keeping going, say, in the middle of your plan when things are getting difficult, try these ideas to remind yourself why you started in the first place.

- Write down the reasons you want to do this and put them where you can see them.
- Think about how you'll be in 2 or 3 years time if you give in now. Write that down and place your list where you can see it to motivate you.
- Think about the advantages of succeeding – better health, better relationships, keeping a job, having more friends, having more fun, having more money, doing better overall. Again, write them down and put them where you can see them.
- Tell as many people as possible what you're doing, so that they can help you (or remind you when you slip).

Ready for some real-life examples?

If you're not sure how to apply the plan to your problem, the next few pages will help.

I WANT TO MAKE NEW FRIENDS

Step 1.

How do you break 'making new friends' into little steps? Change it to 'make *one* new friend'. It's a lot easier to work at finding and connecting with one person than to try to transform yourself into the life and soul of the neighbourhood.

So let's say your chosen step is 'Find and make one new friend'. You can always repeat the process when you've succeeded.

Step 2.

Here's how your brainstorm might go:

- List the people you know already that you'd like to be a friend.
- List the people who you haven't spoken to or hung out with for a while.
- Stop eating alone in the canteen and sit with other people.
- Ask people you know to introduce you to other people.
- Join a club or society.

Step 3.

Let's choose idea 1 (List the people you know already that you'd like to be a friend) and make a plan.

- Look up the phone numbers, email and street addresses of old friends.
- Make a list of the people who you met briefly and those who you added on Instagram or swapped numbers with but have never contacted.
- If you have no way of contacting them but you know their name, add them on Instagram with a friendly message. Now take a look at those whose numbers you do have, and those who are already your Instagram friends.
- Choose one person and text or call them up, or send them a message on Instagram. Invite them to study with you, go for coffee or go for a walk. If they are someone you know from work or college, ask them a question about a difficult piece of work.
- Repeat this process with the next person on your list.

Step 4.

Check the plan (see pages 158-159) and if you have 5 ticks, go for it.

And remember, if this plan doesn't work out, or it gets too much for you in the middle, don't beat yourself up, just go back to the brainstorm and pick another idea to try!

You can do it!

I NEED TO HELP MY CHILD REVISE FOR EXAMS

Step 1.

Almost everyone gets worried about exams- so much to do, so many subjects to revise that it's hard to know where to get started.

This is where the chunking idea is really handy. Don't try and revise everything, just do one subject at a time. So the chunks could be: History / Geography / English / Maths / Science…and so on. What chunk to choose? Let's say History – So that's Step 1.

Step 2.

A brainstorm about ways to revise History could come up with ideas like these:

- Get a copy of the History syllabus and read the topics one by one with your child.
- Make a timetable so that you cover everything by the exam.
- Find a friend who's doing the same exam and they could work together.
- Divide the week into revision periods and don't go out or watch TV at those times.
- Decide on three days a week for revision and encourage them to turn their phone off or leave it with you at those times.
- Pitch a tent in the garden so they can do all their revision in there, away from the TV.
- Go to the library and get some books out about revision technique.
- Go and stay with a relative who only has a black & white TV.

Step 3.

Let's say they choose idea 3 – find a friend and work together. This is what their plan could include:

- Call their friends in the same class, one by one, and outline the idea.
- Do a deal with the first one who agrees.
- Get together and decide on a day to start work
- Decide on a place to work
- Discuss the revision methods they will use- e.g. testing each other?
- Have a plan for when motivation fades.
- Discuss and agree a system of small rewards for good work. Maybe go to the cinema once a week.

Step 4.

Check the plan for 5 ticks and put it into action. And remember, they will need motivation, especially when they've done the first couple of subjects and are switching to a topic they don't like. Here are some of the things you could stick on the wall to remind them why they're doing this:

- Better exam results mean a better career and more money.
- Bad exam results mean little choice of what they do in life.
- Bad exam results only mean they'll have to do it all again next year.
- Most people flunk exams through not working.
- They'll feel great when you've done each subject and feel you've done yourself justice.
- Also, they should plan something good to look forward to after the exams.

You can do it!

NOW IT'S YOUR TURN!

As the real life examples show, the Easy 4-Step Plan works really well. All you have to do is take it step by step and be steady and determined.

If one of the ready-made plans you've just seen fits the bill, please use it!

If you need to make one for yourself, get that piece of paper now and start breaking your elephant into bits!

You can get added advice and support by working through the free linked online modules at www.llttf.com. When you've sorted out your current problem, you might want to choose another chapter and work on something else in your life.

Remember to work on your problem bit by bit using the Easy 4-Step and Planner sheets to plan each step one at a time (remember that poor elephant!).
You can download more worksheets for free from www.llttf.com.

Go for it!

Introduction to Chapter 6

We probably all would like to think we deal with life's challenges in effective and planned ways. Taking the long view and making the healthy choice. But also, if we're honest, that's not always the case. There may be decisions that we each make that make sense as a short term fix, but which come back to cause problems down the line.

There are many choices in life. Some of the most important choices are around when is there too much of a good thing. Think about ice-cream. A single cone is great. Maybe a double cone with the sprinkles on top? Or you could add a chocolate flake? But how many ice-creams can you have at once without feeling sick? Two? Four? What about 24?

There are other life examples like this where something can be healthy, normal and a good thing to do in moderation. So, if someone wants to ask the opinion of a trusted friend about some piece of work they have done, that can be really helpful – and provide useful and constructive feedback. But what if someone starts to feel anxious and doubts themselves and what they do. As a result they start to ask all their friends what they think. They doubt their own choice and keep changing things based on others opinions. Soon their confidence drops even more and they fall into a cycle of seeking reassurance again and again. To start with, their friends are happy to comment, but that good will wears thin when the same question is asked for the 17th time that day.

There are lots of other life choices like this- where the key is to decide how to make sensible choices about what we do. This chapter will help you discover what makes a choice helpful or unhelpful, and help you identify early signs that difficulties are occurring.

Above all, remember, you have choices to make as to how you choose to respond – helpfully or unhelpfully. Your choice.

Chapter 6

THE THINGS YOU DO THAT MESS YOU UP

(and how to stop doing them)

HIDING
AWAY

Eating for
Comfort

Drinking
alcohol

Spending too much

Hitting out at people

Checking
again and
again

BEING
CLINGY

COMPLAINING

TAKING
RISKS

Gossiping

Seeking reassurance all the time

If it makes me feel better, why should I stop?

"Just leave me alone" or "What I need now is chocolate!" We've all said it, and most of the time it's not a problem at all.

But when you're feeling down, the things that get you through can also become the things that mess you up.

Being alone ends up isolating us. One bar of chocolate becomes a comfort eating habit. One drink becomes a whole bottle. One scratch becomes a cycle of risky self-harm. One question "Are you still my friend?" becomes a constant need for reassurance.

And instead of getting better, you get worse.

But this doesn't need to happen! Turn the page and you'll be taking the first step towards getting in control of the things you do.

YOU'RE ON YOUR WAY!

The first step is the most important

And you just took it. You made the decision to stop letting unhelpful behaviours mess up your life.

Now, we're going to help you work out what you're doing too much of, and then show you a simple 4-step way to stop or cut down.

How do you know when something is messing you up?

Turn over

IT AIN'T WHAT YOU DO, IT'S HOW MUCH YOU DO IT

We're not here to be killjoys. There's nothing wrong with chocolate, spending some time alone, or a bit of retail therapy.

But when you're feeling low, you can start to lean on these things, using them to help get you through a bad time.

Other, not so obvious behaviours can also be 'props'. Like hitting out at people – physically or by shouting. Hurting yourself in different ways. Hiding away from the world.

Trouble is, too much of this kind of stuff makes you worse, not better. You get into a kind of vicious cycle, doing something that seems to help for a bit, but finding that it actually makes life worse in the long run.

Are you doing too much of something?

Drinking	2 or 3 drinks a week	More than 2 or 3 a week but not getting drunk
Eating for comfort	Eating chocolate etc. occasionally	Eating a little when you feel upset
Spending Too Much	Buying some things you just fancy	Buying some things that stretch you financially
Taking risks	Seeing occasional risks as fun	You start to "up the stakes" to more dangerous risks
Complaining	You say clearly what you feel and need	You moan a lot that "It's not fair"
Being clingy	You lack some confidence at times	You want others to make important decisions for you
Hitting out at people	You're sometimes rude when frustrated	You begin to throw your weight around
Gossiping	You tell others good news about your friends	You discuss good news told in confidence
Shoplifting	Your friends say they shoplift and you don't tell them it's wrong	You're with friends when they steal and don't say anything
Hiding away	You tend to be quiet in conversations	You avoid spending time with people

A drink every day, sometimes getting drunk	Getting really drunk when you're down	Getting drunk every day
Eating a lot when you feel upset	Bingeing on food when you're upset	Bingeing and making yourself sick when you're upset
Getting into debt – but under control	Spending far more than comes in each week – ignoring the consequences	Run out of credit, paralysed and overwhelmed by debt
You start to get minor injuries	You do things that would put you in hospital if they went wrong	You do things that could be fatal for you or others
You get really upset if you don't get your own way	You get really worked up and upset others too	You are so upset you don't get on with other things and fall out with everyone
You ask other people's opinions all the time	You need others to be near you to feel okay	Your confidence is shot - you can't face anything alone
You often hurt people you don't like	You hit out at people you love when you feel frustrated	You get into fights often - hurting people and being injured yourself
You love to discuss people's private secrets	You get a reputation as someone who can't be trusted	No-one trusts you and you feel lonely
You take something small and say "it's no big deal"	You steal bigger and bigger things more and more often	Your shop-lifting continues and you start to steal in other ways too
You cross the road to avoid chats with people you know	You lose confidence and find it hard even knowing where to start a conversation	You stay in all the time feeling anxious, panicky and depressed

Want to stop or cut down? **Turn over!**

OK.
SO YOU
NEED TO
WORK ON
SOMETHING

Here's how...

First, don't beat yourself up. Most people get into a cycle of doing unhelpful things when they're feeling down. It's bad for you, and often for other people too.

The fact that you're reading this means you're on the way to fixing it.

All you have to do is choose one problem behaviour to work on, and follow our Easy 4-Step Plan (E4SP for short) to get control.

First choose a problem

The Things You Do That Mess You Up

Are you:

	Tick	
Are you eating too many sweet things?	☐	
Sitting around all day?	☐	
Spending too much or little?	☐	
Are you taking any tablets as prescribed?	☐	
Keeping worries to yourself?	☐	
Looking to others for help all the time?	☐	
Lashing out at people?	☐	
Trusting people you don't really know?	☐	
Are you overdoing the phone calls?	☐	
Hiding away?	☐	

	Tick
Being impulsive about important things?	
Setting yourself up to fail/ be rejected?	
Becoming a TV/Internet addict?	
Wanting others to sort out every problem?	
Doing, doing, doing?	
Drinking too much alcohol/ coffee/cola to pick yourself up?	
Sleeping in the whole day?	
Putting things off?	
Worrying all the time?	

Other: please write any other things you do that mess you up here

This way to something good 181

NOW CHOOSE SOMETHING TO DO THAT HELPS

Choose a sensible response

Just one tiny change to what you do and how you react can make all the difference.

Like what?

Well, how about planning and preparing for a good night's sleep. Or why not try doing something that gives you a boost, such as a hobby, having a relaxing bath, or listening to music? Pick something that you think you might feel motivated to do, and of course something that you think you could keep working at.

There are many helpful things that you could do. Choose one or more that you might do instead of the things you do that mess you up.

Helpful things checklist ahead!

The Things You Do That Help

Are you:

Eating regularly and healthily?

Tick ☐

Giving yourself time to sleep?

Tick ☐

Keeping up with routine things like keeping up with the house?

Tick ☐

Doing things with other people?

Tick ☐

Doing things that cheer you up?

Tick ☐

Sharing problems with trusted friends and family?

Tick ☐

Finding out more about how you feel?

Tick ☐

Letting upsetting thoughts just be?

Tick ☐

linked worksheet www.llttf.com

	Tick
Facing your fears?	
Doing exercise/going for walks/ swimming etc?	
Using your sense of humour to cope?	
Planning time for you as well as for others?	
Regularly taking the medicine prescribed by your doctor?	
Relaxing - with music, a film, a book or whatever works for you?	
Asking for help from people around you?	
Doing the essentials like paying bills?	

Q: Am I doing other things that help? Write in what you are doing if this applies to you?

Now, use the Easy 4 Step plan to make changes.

E4SP this way

185

Break the problem into pieces

It's hard to stop doing something all at once, especially if you've been doing it for ages, so break it into easy chunks.

So, if you've lost your confidence and are hiding away from the world, what could you do? You could break the week into bits and decide to do something with someone else on Mondays, for example.

Don't try and become a party animal yet - just work on a little bit of the problem - like getting out of the house.

Or if you're spending too much, start by just cutting out online shopping.

Most problems can be chopped up like this, and you're much more likely to succeed when you do things bit by bit.

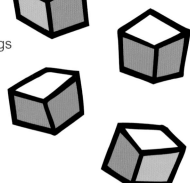

Brainstorm ways to do the first piece

Grab a piece of paper and write down all the things you could do to work on the first bit of the problem.

To meet up with somebody on Mondays, for example, you could ask a friend round, meet one or more people somewhere quiet and comfortable, or try something small like an email, phone call or text. Do anything that reconnects you to others and moves things on.

The trick is to be creative and let your mind go. Write everything down - the ridiculous things as well as the sensible ones.

Do this and there's bound to be a good idea in there somewhere.

TURN OVER FOR STEPS 3 & 4

Phone or text a friend

meet just one person

meet a few

Choose an idea and make a plan to do it

Look at your list of ideas and pick one that looks do-able.
Remember, to make a big change in your life you are best
chunking this into a series of smaller pieces. Make sure
that the steps are small, straightforward and seem like
things you could really do.
Choose something that is:
- Useful for understanding or changing how you are.
- Specific, so that you will know when you have done it.
- Realistic, practical and achievable.
Make each step as small as you like.

Now plan out what you'll do and when.
- *What* are you going to do?
- *When* are you going to do it?
Make sure your plan doesn't push you too far or too fast.
Make it slow and easy to do so you move forward step by
step.
Going to meet on Monday? You need to get it sorted a day
or so before. On the Saturday, text your friend and ask
them round on Monday evening. Ask them to let you know
if they can make it, or whether another time is better.

What if something gets in the way?

As soon as you've written your plan, think about what
could stop it happening. Is there anything that might trip
you up?
- What could arise, and how can you
overcome any problems?
When you know what could block your
progress, make a mini-plan for getting round
the block. This way, you'll be ready for
whatever happens!

Check the plan and put it into action

This is it! You've made your plan, now you need to check that it's do-able. Use this checklist:

Is it realistic?
You're not planning to run a marathon are you?

Are you aiming at just one thing?
Don't try and do more than one item on your list. You can always pick another when you've sorted out the first one.

Is it slow?
There's no need to rush at things. Your plan can take as long as you like, so long as you stick to it, step by step.

Is it easy?
Make your steps small and easy and you'll be more likely to do them.

Are you ready to unblock it?
Have you thought about what could go wrong and how to deal with it?

FIVE TICKS?

THEN GO FOR IT!

NOW KEEP IT GOING!

Just take it step by step

Even a problem that seems huge can be tackled with the E4SP. The secret is breaking everything down into small, manageable pieces.

When you're making your plan, be sure that the steps are small and do-able. Plan to cut down unhelpful behaviours and replace them with helpful one's.

When you're doing your plan, take it step by step and if things get scary in the middle, give yourself a rest or a breather. If it seems too much- take a step back and do something a bit easier for a time.

Then get back on track, until you've put your plan into action.

Be steady and determined, use the E4SP and you will be able to stop doing the things that mess you up, and build more helpful responses.

Use the Planner sheet on the next two pages to help you plan these changes.

Go for it!

Make a plan!

Planner Sheet

1. What am I going to do?

2. When am I going to do it?

3. What problems or difficulties could arise, and how can I overcome them?

Is my planned task -

	Yes	No
Q. Useful for understanding or changing how I am?	☐	☐
Q. Specific, so that I will know when I have done it?	☐	☐
Q. Realistic, practical and achievable?	☐	☐

Introduction to Chapter 7

Do you always stay calm? Relaxed when someone tramples mud onto your carpet? Happy when someone says something bad about you to others? Unless you're a Saint (and we think even Saints lose their tempers sometimes!) there will probably be things every day or every week that make us feel annoyed.

Anger can sometimes be appropriate. If something unjust happens it's entirely healthy and normal to get annoyed – things like poverty, injustice, inequality ... the list goes on of things we should all be angry about. However whether that anger is productive and helpful is also about the choices we make in how we respond.

How we choose to respond when we feel annoyed really matters. Do we lose control and throw a tantrum? Do we shout, or swear or lash out? When we lose control like that we might feel powerful for a time- but in the longer term we can end up becoming isolated. People move away and give us a wide berth, they may be wary of us, and we can feel bad because we lost it rather than responding maturely.

So, how can we slow things down when we start to get angry so we respond in better ways? Mature ways that solve problems rather than adding to them? Again, it involves choices – choices to respond differently. This chapter tells you how to do this and gain control so your anger works for you rather than against you.

Chapter 7

ARE YOU STRONG ENOUGH TO KEEP YOUR TEMPER?

(for times when you feel irritable and angry)

Don't laugh at me

Turn that music down!

She just pushes my buttons

GOT A PROBLEM WITH THAT?

You never listen

DON'T ANSWER ME BACK

YOU MAKE ME DO THIS!

Are you looking at me?

He was asking for it

DON'T TALK TO ME LIKE THAT!

He really winds me up

Excuses, excuses

What 'reason' do you use when you fly off the handle?

Did someone else say something, do something or forget to do something? Maybe you got into an argument and the other person wouldn't listen. Did a family member or a neighbour make too much noise? Was it your child, brother, sister or friend that pushed your buttons?

Whatever your excuse, and however much you feel like lashing out at the time, the truth is, getting angry gets you nowhere.

Except into trouble, into hospital, and out of relationships. Lose your temper all the time and you'll probably lose everything, eventually.

And anyway, temper tantrums are for kids.

They're what you do when you lose it. When all you can think of is throwing your toys out of the pram. When you don't know the difference between being strong and being aggressive.

Know what we think?

197

IT'S WEAK TO STAY AND ARGUE

Doesn't sound right, does it?

A lot of people say that standing your ground is strong, that you should look up to people who don't take any nonsense.

But think about it. What happens when you lose your temper? Things get out of control and you get into trouble. People steer clear of you. You end up on your own.

What's so strong about that?

Wouldn't it be better NOT to shout and lash out? Wouldn't it be better to be admired for being calm and in control?

This chapter can help you do that, but you'll have to be strong. A lot stronger than your angry self.

Strong stuff next →

IT'S STRONG TO KEEP YOUR COOL

Get a different plan

Strong, calm, controlled people choose to avoid aggravation in the first place, or they choose to react differently when they feel their hackles start to rise.

It takes real strength to do this. It's much easier to lose it, shout or swear, stamp your feet or throw a punch.

But this chapter will help you take the tougher option. When you use the 3-step plan that comes later, you'll really get to know your own temper and how to keep it under control.

You'll become calmer, quieter, more powerful. And the people who count will know that you're a much stronger person than you used to be.

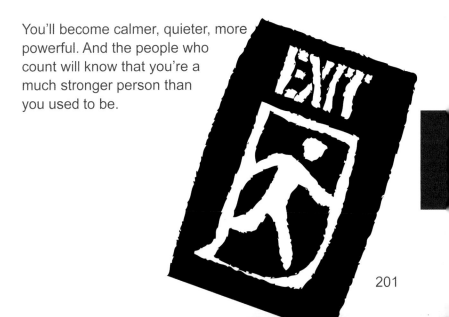

YOU GOT A PROBLEM WITH THAT?

It's not strong to lose it

If you still think losing control of yourself isn't stupid, think about this:

Imagine you're driving a fast car and you come to a tight bend with a slippery surface. You're going to need all your skill to stay on the road, so you take a deep breath, remember everything you've learned about driving, grip the wheel and control the car until the danger is past.

What would happen if you lost it, instead? If you let a red mist come down and you got angry at the bend because it was too tight? You'd skid, wouldn't you? You, the car and your passengers would end up in the ditch, in the hospital or in the graveyard.

In your life, you're always in that car. Your aim is to finish your journey in one piece. That slippery bend is just something that 'pushes your buttons'.

Use your skill to stay in control. Lose your temper and you don't.

Lost it!

Now ask what's in it for you

WHAT'S IN IT FOR ME?

Big respect

The self-respect you earn when you stay in control and use your skill and strength to handle a tough situation.

The respect of your friends and family who look at you in a new way and start to realise that you're stronger than they thought.

The respect of strangers who, when you speak calmly or walk away from angry situations, know that you helped to make things better, not worse.

There's not much that's more important than making good decisions. If you agree, and think you're strong enough to try our 3-step plan, turn the page and…

Let's get started!

IT'S EASY TO BE STRONG

As easy as...

Know your buttons

Think about what makes you angry. The people or places that always seem to get you going. When you know your buttons, you can keep them from being pressed.

Know your early warning system

You feel different just before you snap. With some people it's heavy breathing. Others feel the blood pounding in their ears. Learn to spot these signs so you can move to step 3 before they turn into trouble.

Know where the escape hatches are

You just decide to react differently this time. Some people pause and count to 10, or decide to walk away. Others have phrases that they say, that de-fuse a situation. When you have a few of these up your sleeve, you'll be able to stay in control whatever happens.

Breathe!

As soon as you've responded differently, give yourself respect. You're strong. You're in control. You've steered the car round that slippery corner without losing it.

You've been strong enough to keep your temper.

So let's do it

KNOW
YOUR
BUTTONS

What always gets you going?

Something someone says at home? What about your friends? Other people? What about when people are noisy around you or tell you what to do?

Is it your brother/sister, a boss, the government, the police, traffic wardens, white vans? Do you suffer from road rage? (Actually, you don't, it's everybody around you that suffers).

What about when you drink. Is it worse then? And when you're having a night out, does just being with your mates make you feel like arguing or fighting?

These are all buttons. You need to think about them so that you know exactly which ones apply to you. Then you need to write them down on the next 2 pages.

FEELING LEFT OUT

BEING TOLD OFF

BEING IGNORED

Why? Because when you know your buttons, you can keep them from being pressed. Go to different places. Spend time with different friends. Ignore other people's comments. Get control of the car, steer round the corner and forget about what other drivers are doing.

This way to the buttons

209

My Buttons

Write down the things that make you lose your temper or get irritable

What gets me going?

linked
worksheet
www.llttf.com

What gets me going?

Step 2 next

KNOW YOUR EARLY WARNING SYSTEM

Feeling tense?

Think about the last time you lost your temper. How did you feel just beforehand? Can you remember what happened, physically or mentally?

You may have started breathing heavily, clenched your fists, stood up suddenly, folded your arms, drummed on the table with your fingers. Some people really do see a red mist in front of their eyes.

Or maybe your early warnings are in your mind. You start to feel critical of someone else. You don't think much of their appearance, their voice, their clothes, their opinions. Maybe you feel ignored or think people are looking down on you.

All these signs are really useful, because they warn you that you're getting near to losing it. They're like a road sign that says 'Slippery corner ahead'.

Think about the signs that apply to you and write down as many as you can on the next two pages.

List this way

1 2 3 Breathe!

My Early Warning System

Write down all the things you think and feel,
just before you lose it

Feeling hot or breathing hard (for example)

What to do when you start to feel this way

USE THE ESCAPE HATCH

This is when you react differently

Here's when you count to 10, or change the subject, or walk away, or sit down, relax your shoulders and breathe deeply.

Some people 'switch on' some music in their head when they get one of their early warning signs.

Others have a few words that they whisper to take the heat out of the situation ('slippery corner, watch the road ahead' are good ones).

You need to have a choice of escape hatches and be ready to use one whenever you get an early warning sign.

You can invent your own, of course, that fit with the buttons you wrote down earlier. Or you can turn the page and see some of the escape hatches that other people use. They won't mind you borrowing them.

More ideas this way

MORE ESCAPE HATCHES

Smile

When your face or fists are tensing up, make yourself smile and feel the aggravations go away. Don't just bare your teeth, give out a proper big smile that lights up your face. Others will notice, and things will calm down.

Say "You might be right about that"

This works best when you really disagree with someone. Instead of arguing and getting angry, just say "You might be right about that". You don't have to mean it, it's an escape hatch. Often, the other person will be so surprised that all the tension will drain away.

Sit down

When we're about to burst, we need to be standing, so we can fight, or run, or seem bigger than we are.

It's a lot harder to get into trouble when you're sitting down though, so when you get an early warning, stay in your seat, or go find one.

Hum

We're serious. What's your favourite song? Get into the habit of humming it to yourself when you get an early warning. Use it to change you focus. It works even better with slow, calming tunes.

And finally

BREATHE

Relax your shoulders and breathe slowly

Often, your shoulders are up around your ears when tension builds. If you notice this in time and make a point of relaxing and letting them drop, you'll calm yourself and others too. Breathe slowly and think about slippery corners while you do it.

When you breathe, close your mouth – it's hard to over-breathe through your nose.

And as you breathe, reconnect with your body and surroundings. Use it to centre yourself – to step back and notice your reactions.

Stop, think and reflect.

Use the breaths to focus and change how you react.

Feels great doesn't it?

1 2 3 Breathe!

SO
NEXT
TIME

Follow the plan

Know your buttons

Get to know the buttons on your list. When you know them, you can keep them from being pressed.

Know your early warning system

Learn your danger signs and look out for them so that you can move to step 3 before they turn into trouble.

Know where the escape hatches are

React differently. Count to 10, walk away, say the phrase, hum the tune. Whatever your chosen escapes are, use one as soon as you get an early warning sign.

Breathe!

Now give yourself respect.

You're powerful. You're in control. You've steered the car round that slippery corner without losing it.

You're strong enough to keep your temper!
Now, time to make a plan. Pick one small thing to practice or change. Then use the Planner sheet on pages 224-225 to give yourself the best start.

Once you're done, use the Review sheet on pages 226-227 to check your progress.

Go, make a plan

Go for it!

Don't just sit there, make a plan!

Planner sheet

1. What am I going to do?

2. When am I going to do it?

3. What problems or difficulties could arise, and how can I overcome them?

Is my planned task -

Q. Useful for improving
   my well-being?

Yes ☐ No ☐

Q. Specific, so that I will
   know when I have done it?

Yes ☐ No ☐

Q. Realistic, practical
   and achievable?

Yes ☐ No ☐

How did it go?

Review Sheet

What did you plan to do? Write it here:

If yes:

1. What went well?

2. What didn't go so well?

3. What have you learned from what happened?

4. How are you going to apply what you have learned?

Did you try to do it?

Yes   **No**

If no: what stopped you?

Internal things (forgot, not enough time, put it off, didn't think I could do it, couldn't see the point etc.).

External things (other people, work or home issues etc.).

How can you tackle things differently next time?

Introduction to Chapter 8

We all want to feel happier don't we? To enjoy things, to feel and live in healthy ways, and to appreciate the good things around us. But sometimes it can seem so hard. This chapter makes a remarkable claim. That there are some things that we can all choose to do which can help start to make us feel happier straight away. Each of the things are small achievable actions that can have powerful impacts on how we feel.

But setting up new habits can feel hard. Think back to the start of the year and all the New Year Resolutions that each of us can make- and often fail to keep. What causes a failed resolution? Being unrealistic? Maybe trying to do it all by yourself? Maybe beating yourself up mentally if you have a setback? There's so many things that can make change hard. That's why this chapter- and each of the other chapters ends with the idea of making a plan. Having a Plan gives you direction. It helps you plan what you'll do and when you'll do it. That pattern of *Plan, Do* and *Review* (using the Planner and Review sheets) is a pattern you can use to take forward the lessons of this chapter, this book and the linked course.

So, as you come to this final topic, remember you have choices and control going forward in your life. Use the Planner and Review sheets to help you make effective plans, so you move forward learning all the time. That way, you really will move towards living life to the full.

Chapter 8

10 THINGS YOU CAN DO TO FEEL HAPPIER STRAIGHT AWAY

(for when you want some practical things to make a difference now)

No Doctors
No Pills
No Booze
No Drugs
No Jogging
No Gym
No Diets
No Supplements
No Preaching
No Pain

You can start feeling better about 10 minutes from now

Like loads of people, you're not feeling great at the moment.

Your system's a bit sluggish. You're miserable some of the time. You think your life could be better all round, but nothing seems to cheer you up these days.

So here's the good news: you can start to feel better in a few minutes from now. All you have to do is finish reading this chapter and then make some small, easy changes to what you do each day.

More good stuff

DON'T PANIC!

No broccoli is involved

You *will* have to get off the couch and walk about a bit. You'll also have to say no to a burger or two, but you won't have to wear Lycra shorts and we promise not to turn you into a vegetarian.

The thing is this: there are things you can do and things you can eat that can *make you feel happier straight away*.

Amazingly, some foods can help you get going to face the day. Some activities give you a major boost – direct to the brain.

When you combine the two – eating and doing certain things – those fed up feelings can improve (along with spots and even excess weight sometimes).

And it's easy. You just make ten small changes to your daily routine.

Are you ready?

10 SMALL, EASY CHANGES

1. The Escalator Business

2. The Banana Thing

3. Put On Your WOW Glasses

4. You Old Smoothie

5. Doing Porridge

6. Heavy Breathing

7. Make A Note Of This

8. Take One Away

9. Do something for someone else

10. The Happy List

This way to small, easy change No.1 →

THE ESCALATOR BUSINESS

Turn your back on lifts and escalators

Exercise is good for you. So good that when you do it, your body says 'thanks' by boosting happy chemicals in your brain.

But who's got the time or money to go to the gym?

Instead, use the stairs rather than the lift or escalator when you're out shopping, at work or at school.

Climbing stairs is one of the best ways there is to get fitter and get that happy stuff into your head. In fact climbing stairs each day for a year is the same as climbing a large mountain. Great view isn't it!

Decide to do it next time you're out. Then decide to keep on doing it and always take the stairs. Your brain will get happier and happier.

While you're climbing the stairs at the shopping centre, here's what to buy…

THE BANANA THING

Monkeys aren't stupid

Did you ever see a depressed chimp?

Not many people know this, but a banana can help produce the same happy chemical in your head as a pill. What's more, they give you a steady supply of energy. And bananas are available off prescription.

Be honest, ways to start to feel a bit better don't get much easier than this.

1. Eat a banana.

2. That's it. Eat the banana.

One a day is good, and here's a way to make those good feelings even stronger – walk to the shops and use the stairs when you go and buy your bananas.

Small, easy change No.3 next

PUT ON YOUR 'WOW' GLASSES

The world is amazing when you really look at it

When was the last time you went outside and really noticed what's there? The wind, the warmth, the cold, the rain, the trees, the flowers, the shops and the sky.

When you stop and think, the world is full of stuff that makes you go 'Wow!'

People who recover from really bad times often say they appreciate things they used to take for granted. So put on your special glasses and see the world for the amazing place it is.

Even better do it with a friend. Go for walks together, talk about good times, and you'll soon get those happy chemicals coursing through your brain!

TEST IT OUT

Use this page to rate your mood before and after your WOW walk.

Use it to discover the effect of your WOW walk on you.

Rate your mood
(Before your walk)

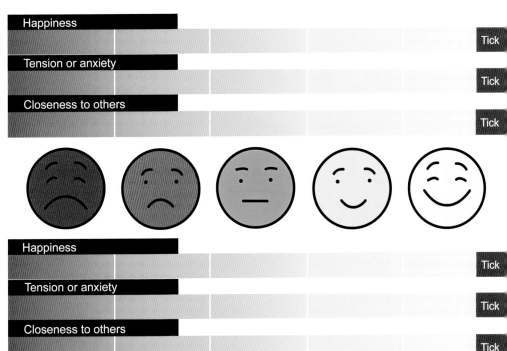

Happiness					Tick
Tension or anxiety					Tick
Closeness to others					Tick

Happiness					Tick
Tension or anxiety					Tick
Closeness to others					Tick

Rate your mood
(After your walk)

YOU OLD SMOOTHIE

Are you fed up with hearing about 5 a day?

Even if you like fruit and vegetables, it's hard to have five portions a day.

Trouble is, you really do need that much fibre. Without it, your system clogs up and you get all sad and sluggish.

So here's a cheat – drink smoothies. They're just mashed up fruit and veg, usually with most of the good stuff left in, and just one glass a day gets you started. Get a blender and make your own to get the variety.

Ready? Walk briskly to the shop, buy the fruit and veg you like. Walk briskly home, mix, mash and enjoy, feel smug.

Got diabetes or watching your weight? Then choose low sugar fruits like berries, cherries, apples, grapefruit, pears, apricots, strawberries, plums and of course bananas (lower sugar especially when they are under-ripe).

DOING PORRIDGE

Breakfast gets you going

It's amazing but it's true. When you do without breakfast, your body doesn't get the right kind of start and it sulks all day, demanding coffee or snacks and often giving you a headache by lunchtime.

But when you eat a bowl of porridge or muesli each morning, you don't need all those snacks, your digestion works better and your day gets off to a great start.

Porridge and muesli work like – how can we put this – drain unblockers. After a few days they clear your system out and you feel better all round.

Walk quickly to the corner shop and buy some, now.

HEAVY BREATHING

Faster, faster

You already exercise. If you do household chores, they're exercise. When you clean the car or do the garden, that's exercise. When you lift or move things at work or school, that's exercise.

So why don't you feel better? Because you're not doing it fast enough. Exercise only works properly and produces happy chemicals when you get out of breath, and your heart starts pumping.

So do the housework faster. Clean the car quicker. Take a brisk walk for 20-30 minutes. Move those files or shift those boxes at a run (always being careful not to take risks or hurt yourself of course).

Oh, and while doing it ...

You could try the next idea

MAKE A NOTE OF THIS

Don't suffer in silence

Music cheers you up. Obvious? So why are you sitting there in silence? Silence is just a space for you to think about your worries in.

Put some of your favourite music on. Do it now. Play music while you're exercising and getting out of breath and it'll send even more happy feelings to your brain.

Play music while you're walking briskly to the shops. Play music while you're sitting around. Create a "happy" playlist for when you need a boost.

But don't play sad stuff, or songs that remind you of unhappy times. Keep it upbeat and you'll get an instant lift.

TAKE
ONE
AWAY

This one saves money too

Eating too much fast food or takeaway food is a great way to get really down.

Did you see that experiment where a man ate nothing but fast food? He felt depressed and really unhealthy inside a couple of weeks.

So here's what you do: cut out one burger or take-away a week. Just one. Replace it with something you make yourself (easy things like beans on toast are fine).

It won't change your life all at once, but put together with the extra exercise and healthier eating you're doing, within a few weeks you'll start to feel lighter, fitter and happier. And a bit better off.

DO SOMETHING FOR SOMEONE ELSE

It ain't what you do, it's who you do it for

Do a small kindness for someone else, every day, and you'll feel even better than they do. What's more, you'll feel good straight away.

It doesn't have to be a big thing like sometimes helping at a soup kitchen or drop-in centre (although those would be great, of course).

You can just as easily get a lift in your mood by helping someone with their work, writing a letter of thanks for being your friend, cooking a meal or spending time with a person who needs the company.

Go on, sit down now and plan one or two helpful things you're going to do for other people this week. They'll feel good, but you'll feel even better!

Final idea coming up next

THE
HAPPY
LIST

My Good Times

Remember the good things

When you're down it's easy to forget the good times- times you've succeeded in something, happy times with friends, things that make you smile and times you did something to help someone else.

So remember them. Each evening, sit down and write down three things that you:

- Have enjoyed.

- Felt was a job well done.

- Or helped you feel close to someone else.

Is there anything to be thankful for? After a few days, you'll have a list of great things that you can look back on, and will help you feel a lot better.

What you think about affects how you feel. Focus on the good things and you'll be happier for it!

Try it out

MY
GOOD
TIMES

Write down all the things you've enjoyed, felt was a job well done, or has helped you feel close to someone else.

How much did it fit with your values/ideals of how you want to live your life? Is there anything you are thankful for?

WHAT ARE YOU WAITING FOR?

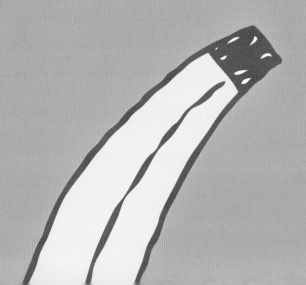

Go and get that banana

At the beginning of this chapter, we promised you could start feeling better in ten minutes. It's time, so here's what to do – make a plan and get going.

Pick one small thing then use the Planner sheet on pages 262-263 to give yourself the best start.

If it's daylight, go out, walk briskly to the corner shop and buy a couple of bananas. Walk quickly home and eat them.

If it's night and the shops are closed, walk up and down your stairs for ten minutes if you're able, or long enough to get your heart pumping.

Whichever you do, you'll know you're making changes that make a difference

Once you're done, use the Review sheet on pages 264-265 to check your progress.

Go for it!

Make a plan!

Planner Sheet

1. What am I going to do?

2. When am I going to do it?

3. What problems or difficulties could arise, and how can I overcome them?

Is my planned task -

Q. Useful for understanding or changing how I am?

Yes ☐ No ☐

Q. Specific, so that I will know when I have done it?

Yes ☐ No ☐

Q. Realistic, practical and achievable?

Yes ☐ No ☐

How did it **go?**

Review Sheet

What did you plan to do? Write it here:

If yes:

1. What went well?

2. What didn't go so well?

3. What have you learned from what happened?

4. How are you going to apply what you have learned?

linked
worksheet
www.llttf.com

Review Day

Did you try to do it?

Yes　　**No**

If no: what stopped you?

Internal things (forgot, not enough time, put it off, didn't think I could do it, couldn't see the point etc.).

External things (other people, work or home issues etc.).

How can you tackle things differently next time?

WHERE TO GET EVEN MORE HELP

(but no broccoli)

For more tips on feeling better, go to www.llttf.com. It's free and the number one site for low mood and anxiety recommended by NHS Trusts and teams in England.* It's packed with ways to lift your mood and start having a happier and healthier life.

There are links on there, too, so you can connect with other people who are making changes to their lives too.

And don't worry, last time we looked, very few vegetables were mentioned.

*Bennion et al, 2017. BMJ Open http://bmjopen.bmj.com/content/7/1/e014844